Derbyshire

Car Tours

John Brooks

Acknowledgements
Heather Pearson and Sandy Sims of the Ordnance Survey provided
invaluable help in checking the text against the maps. My son, Josh, was
an excellent and patient driver and I am also grateful for the advice
offered by staff at libraries and Tourist Information Centres throughout
the county.

Front cover photograph: *Dove Dale*
Title page photograph: *Chatsworth House*

Author: John Brooks
Series Editor: Anne-Marie Edwards
Editors: Stephen Larden, Donald Greig
Designers: Brian Skinner, Ellen Moorcraft
Photographs: Jarrold Publishing

Ordnance Survey   ISBN 0-3190-0627-1
Jarrold Publishing   ISBN 0-7117-0847-9

First published 1996 by Ordnance Survey and Jarrold Publishing

Ordnance Survey   Jarrold Publishing
Romsey Road   Whitefriars
Maybush   Norwich NR3 1TR
Southampton SO16 4GU

Printed in Great Britain by Jarrold Book Printing, Thetford, Norfolk 1/96

CONTENTS

INTRODUCTION TO DERBYSHIRE

Main roads only give a hint of the beauty of Derbyshire's scenery. The busy traffic, with heavy lorries seeming to predominate, often makes leisurely driving impractical, and it is only when you escape to lesser roads that you can begin to appreciate the quality of the landscape at a proper pace.

Few English counties of comparable size can rival Derbyshire's variety of landscapes, which range from the flat and fertile Trent basin in the south to the heathery moorland of the Dark Peak to the north. Within these extremes lie nearly a thousand square miles of diverse countryside. It must be admitted that not all of it has the outstanding quality shown in the Peak National Park, but even the most mundane parts usually compensate with interesting historical connections or examples of outstanding architecture. It must be remembered that throughout history Derbyshire has been a cradle of industrial development and this has inevitably left its mark on the landscape with the many features which delight industrial archaeologists. Nevertheless humble byways present unexpected beauty such as verges of waist-high cow parsley in front of thorn hedges frothing with May blossom.

'The Peak District' are words which immediately bring Derbyshire to mind, which is rather unfair as considerable areas belong to Staffordshire, Cheshire and Yorkshire as well. The Dark Peak is the most northerly geological and geographical division of the Peak District, being the large horseshoe-shaped area of highland composed of gritstone and shale which surrounds the limestone dales on every side except the south. The latter are the southernmost part of the Peak District and you have to prefix 'Derbyshire' to distinguish them from the ones in Yorkshire.

Chrome and Parkhouse Hills from Earl Sterndale

The gritstone of the Dark Peak weathers in a different way from limestone, leaving eccentrically eroded summits and ridges like those of the Roaches or Froggatt Edge. To check whether you are in a limestone or gritstone area look at the stone walls – limestone is white or light grey and irregular in shape while gritstone is significantly darker and the stones are often flatter. The

The Hope Valley from Higger Tor, Hathersage

White Peak is the name given to the limestone area to the south of the Dark Peak and it thus includes the dales within its limits. This is the southernmost end of the Pennines, the highland spine of northern England which extends to the Cheviot heights on the Scottish border.

Southern Derbyshire is a less spectacular area too often neglected by visitors to the county. Kedleston, Calke, and Hardwick are National Trust properties, each of them providing unique insights into the way of life of the county's landed gentry in times past. Calke Abbey is particularly interesting. Here an almost feudal way of life continued into the twentieth century and this is reflected in the furnishings and atmosphere of the house. Hedges enclose the fields of south Derbyshire rather than stone walls, and there are villages of snug cottages surrounding church and pub in the traditional way. The area also includes Derby and other industrial conurbations which grew up around the coalfield, but most people coming here today, and remembering the district from twenty or thirty years ago, will be amazed at the way that the landscape is recovering from the effects of mining and heavy industry. The outlook from Bolsover Castle and Sutton Scarsdale Hall is immeasurably improved, and this is a degree of compensation for the decline in employment from industries which had flourished for a hundred and fifty years and more. Chatsworth House and Haddon Hall are Derbyshire's prime heritage attractions and both lie within the National Park.

Industrial Development

Derby saw the birth of the industrial revolution with the opening of the world's first factory in 1717. This was the silk mill built by John Lombe on the banks of the River Derwent which was the precursor of the innumerable textile mills which were to be built by Derbyshire's fast-flowing rivers. The tall, gaunt shells of these buildings are a distinctive feature of the scenery in far-flung corners of the county, from remote Edale in the north to Belper in the south (where one of Jedediah Strutt's original mills is still used by a cotton- spinning company). Chesterfield, in the north-east of the county, was a quiet country town until the expansion of the coalfield led to its transformation in the nineteenth century into a centre of heavy industry. Consequently its character changed and many of its medieval and Georgian buildings were destroyed. It is now beginning to revert to its former role as a busy market centre serving much of north-east Derbyshire.

Mining was the earliest of Derbyshire's industries with the extraction of copper and lead being established before the arrival of the Romans. Many hillsides in the peaks and dales still bear the scars of shallow shafts sunk in medieval times, but occasionally there are more substantial remains of the lead mines which operated in comparatively recent times. The Magpie Mine at Sheldon is probably the best-known of these, with its handsome engine house and chimney so reminiscent of a Cornish tin mine. This mine was one of the last to operate and finally closed in the 1950s. In the eighteenth and nineteenth centuries lead mining was an ideal complement to the spinning and weaving of cotton which occupied women and children either at home or in the mills while the menfolk of the family worked in the mines. This could be extremely hazardous as, for instance, when three men were suffocated in Magpie Mine in 1833. It was said that they were racing to drive a shaft towards a rich vein of ore in

Quarrying

It is ironic that now that the scars made by old lead workings are becoming lost in the landscape, an extraction industry has grown up to rework the waste from the abandoned mines. Fluorspar (fluoride of calcium) is vital to the steel and chemical industries and was discarded as 'gangue' by the lead miners. Some of these old spoilheaps are now being reworked but fortunately not all of the workings are on the surface. A mine now established at Great Hucklow has the advantage that the waste can infill worked-out passages rather than be dumped on the surface. Barytes is another mineral refined from old limestone workings and is used in the paint and oil industries.

Limestone quarrying is far more of a problem and this has eaten into hillsides all over the White Peak. The tall chimney of the cement works in the Hope Valley is a landmark as well known as Mam Tor itself. Peak District limestone is exceptionally pure and thus makes excellent cement. Unfortunately many of the quarries do not produce it for this purpose but sell it as an aggregate for road-making and other construction work. The National Park regards this as the waste of a natural resource which is also detrimental to many fine landscapes. On the other hand quarrying provides employment for a large number of local people and many subsidiary industries have grown up in its wake.

This beautifully preserved steam engine was once used to haul wagons up to the summit of Middleton Top

competition with a neighbouring mine, and the rival miners lit a fire whose smoke filled the Magpie workings. This confirmed the mine's reputation for being cursed and unlucky, and a ghost known as the Old Man haunted its soughs (drainage tunnels) and passages.

Feasts and Customs

The Old Man of the Magpie Mine is far from being Derbyshire's only ghost and the usual headless horsemen and phantom black dogs abound, as do some more unusual spectres such as the phantom helicopter which haunted the skies around Buxton during the winter of 1973–74. However, ghosts never appear to order and those with a taste for folklore and 'the old beliefs' are better served by the ancient ceremonies which survive in many places. The best-known of these are the well-dressings, which seem to have their origins in a pagan custom. In the seventeenth century this form of thanksgiving was revived when water remained in the wells even after a prolonged summer drought. However, the praise was now directed towards Jesus and God the Father rather than the water gods of the heathens.

Today well-dressings take place in all parts of Derbyshire and further afield throughout spring and summer, and the tableaux, intricately-worked with flower petals, moss, etc. and held in a frame of wet clay, usually depict religious subjects.

Derbyshire folk have never turned down the chance of a good party and many of the old customs surviving in the towns and villages also provide an excuse for downing a pint or two. Earl Sterndale provides the most blatant example of this where the man found to be most drunk on the day before the annual Wakes begin was elected mayor of the village for a year. At Ashbourne the Shrovetide football match has been held since the fifteenth century, play flowing from one side of the town to the other in a game where the ball is seldom kicked and more usually held in a perpetual scrimmage. Here too a good deal of ale is drunk in the course of the day. Castleton keeps 29 May (Oak Apple Day) as a feast and calls it Garland Day. In theory the festivities commemorate the restoration of Charles II but some believe that their origins lie in a pagan fertility rite celebrating the arrival of summer. The garland is a richly-decorated frame which covers the body of a horseman down to the waist. He is the king of the Garlanding and, dressed in seventeenth-century clothes, leads a procession which goes round the village and ends at the church, where the garland is hauled to the top of the tower and tied to a pinnacle.

Church clipping is a much less riotous custom which displays parishioners' love for their place of worship. Wirksworth has a particularly beautiful church and on the Sunday nearest to 8 September the congregation leave the church and form a circle around it, holding hands to embrace the building symbolically. A similar event takes place at Burbage church on the outskirts of Buxton. A service known as a Lovefeast takes place each year on the first Sunday in July in an exceptionally remote location. This is held in a barn at Alport Castles Farm, just to the north of the Snake Pass. When non-conformists were being persecuted in the seventeenth century, secret services were held in lonely places like this. Later, John Wesley preached at the barn and the Lovefeast continues the tradition though congregations are said to be dwindling.

The Padley Chapel at Grindleford was originally the gatehouse of a medieval mansion belonging to the Fitzherbert family. They were ardent Catholics and in 1588 two priests were discovered in the house. The

Chesterfield well-dressing

The mill pond at Cromford, a village created by Richard Arkwright in 1771

priests were taken to Derby and hanged, drawn and quartered while the Fitzherberts forfeited their estate. In 1933 the gatehouse, which had become very dilapidated, was bought by the Catholic diocese of Nottingham and made into a chapel to commemorate the two martyrs. A pilgrimage takes place there each year on the Thursday nearest to 20 July and a special mass is celebrated on the following Sunday.

Early Tourists

Edward Browne, son of the famous philosopher Sir Thomas Browne, was one of the first travellers to leave a written account of a tour of Derbyshire. He wrote in 1662 of the difficulties encountered in exploring this '…strange, mountainous, misty, moorish, rocky, wild country…the craggy ascents, the rocky uneveness of the roade, the high peaks and the almost perpendicular descents…'. Celia Fiennes echoed these feelings in 1697: 'All Derbyshire is full of steep hills, and nothing but the peakes of hills as thick one by another is seen in most of the County which are very steepe which makes travelling tedious, and the miles long…'. This intrepid explorer was riding sidesaddle on rough and unmapped tracks, attempting to travel as quickly as possible between houses to which she had introductions. She complained that it was no use asking the way from locals since '…the common people know not above 2 or 3 mile from their home.' Thirty years later Daniel Defoe journeyed through the county and invited readers to travel with him '…through this howling wilderness in your imagination, and you shall soon find all that is wonderful about it.' Defoe's romantic view of Derbyshire appealed to the notion of the picturesque fashionable in the eighteenth century. Buxton and Matlock developed as spas at the end of the eighteenth century and the appeal of their health-restoring waters was enhanced by their proximity to inspiring scenery. The coming of the railway brought new visitors to the peaks and dales. Mill workers and miners flocked to the countryside on Sundays and Bank Holidays and made Derbyshire a playground where they could enjoy grand scenery and fresh air. In more recent times many people will have fond memories of a school trip to the Peak District to learn about geography and geology. While the lessons may have been forgotten, the splendour of the scenery will have stayed in the mind and the visit may well have generated a love of landscape and walking which will last a lifetime.

Dove Dale in winter

The Peak National Park

By Roland Smith,
Head of Information Services,
Peak National Park

The Peak has always been an important lung for the surrounding cities and towns whose residents make up half the population of England. Generations of Manchester mill-workers and Sheffield steelmen have looked up at the misty blue outline of the Peak District moors knowing that at the weekend, for the cost of a short bus ride, they could be tramping freely across those heights.

But before the Peak National Park came into existence as the first in Britain in 1951, many of the highest and wildest of those inviting moors were barred to walkers by owners and gamekeepers, who kept them sacrosanct for the raising and shooting of grouse. Ribbon development and quarrying activities were also biting into this last remaining 'wilderness' between Manchester and Sheffield.

Trespassing on the forbidden moors of Kinder Scout and Bleaklow became something of a growth sport for ramblers from those surrounding cities in the 1920s and 1930s. Things came to a head with the notorious Mass Trespass on 24 April, 1932, when five ramblers were sentenced to prison after some minor scuffles with gamekeepers in William Clough, near Hayfield.

Although such direct action was frowned upon by the official ramblers' federations at the time, the Mass Trespass became an important catalyst and rallying-point for the campaign for National Parks and access to the countryside. After the Dower and Hobhouse Reports had highlighted the need for National Parks, the post-war Labour Government enacted the 1949 National Parks and Access to the Countryside Act, which laid the foundation for the present system.

The Peak was the first National Park to be designated in April

1951 because, for the reasons stated above, it was a national park where it was most needed. One of the first acts of the new Peak Park Planning Board was to start negotiations with landowners to allow free access to those moorlands which were the scene of the access battles of the 1930s.

Today, over 80 square miles of moorland in the north and east of the Park is covered by access agreements, allowing the rambler free access for most of the year, subject to a common-sense set of bye-laws. It is still a Mecca for the walker, with over 1,600 miles of public footpaths and rights of way and an astonishing variety of scenery.

The Peak National Park covers 555 square miles between Dove Dale in the south and Holmfirth in the north, and 38,000 people live within its boundaries. The job of the National Park Authority, which controls development in the area, is to conserve and enhance this protected landscape, and to provide recreational opportunities and promote understanding among its millions of visitors. The interests of local people are always taken into account, and the Park's Ranger Service acts as an important link between them and the visitors.

ENJOY YOUR TOUR

Please read through the tour before starting, and if visibility is poor when you intend to set out then reject one that offers fine panoramas from lofty viewpoints in favour of a neighbouring route that visits historic buildings or towns. Note that all routes are circular so they can be started at any point. Tour instructions are in bold type. There are also boxed letters which correspond to those on the map. Their purpose is to aid your navigation and, in many instances, highlight sections of the route requiring particular attention. The times given for each tour cover motoring only; if you decide to explore footpaths or visit attractions, they can easily take the best part of a day. The opening times of the various attractions can change, and you are advised to telephone and check before visiting. If you plan more extensive walks the Pathfinder guides and Pathfinder maps at 1:25,000 scale (2½ inches to 1 mile, 4cm to 1km) are ideal. For details see inside back cover.

In order to explore some of the loveliest areas of the Peak District many of the routes here follow narrow roads with steep gradients. Some cross high ground and may be blocked by drifting snow or made hazardous by ice in winter (gritting trucks rarely venture off the main roads). Obviously, driving on minor roads in hill country presents problems not encountered elsewhere. It is always best to assume that there is a slow-moving tractor just around the next bend, and to keep a lookout for sheep or cattle that might stray on to the (often unfenced) road. Never trust roadside sheep and lambs who may appear to be preoccupied with grazing – they are likely to amble across the road at the last minute. And finally, if you are sightseeing on a single-track road, please remember to pull over into the passing places as often as possible to allow following traffic to pass.

SOUTH WINGFIELD AND ILAM FROM MATLOCK

61 MILES – 3 HOURS
START AND FINISH AT MATLOCK

This tour combines countryside that will be familiar to many people (Dove Dale and the Manifold Valley, for instance) with lesser-known landscapes like that of the Amber Valley. South Wingfield Manor will be the highlight of the route for many people, and the National Tram Museum at Crich, Lea Gardens and Ilam Country Park are also on the drive.

Take the A615 eastwards out of Matlock to head for Alfreton and pass the cinema. Riber Castle is facing you on the hill ahead and there are colourful gardens to the right. The road passes the football and cricket grounds. **Just beyond the traffic lights turn right to Starkholmes.** This road climbs steeply past Old Matlock church to the right and was the coach road out of Matlock in the eighteenth century. The hill must have taxed the strength of the horses. **At the end of the village, just beyond the post office, turn left up the very steep Riber Road which has sharp hairpin bends.** The driver should take care not to be distracted by the panoramic views to the Heights of Abraham and Matlock Bath.

When the road levels bear right down Carr Lane (the way ahead goes to Riber Castle Wildlife Park). **After 300 yards turn right down Littlemoor Lane following the sign to Lea and Holloway.** This is a lovely byway through well-wooded countryside. A road leaves to the left to Dethick. **Keep on here** but at the next junction turn left into Lea up Baker's Lane. Go straight over the main road A at the top of the hill into Long Lane following a sign to Lea Gardens which are about 300 yards along this lane on the right.

Beyond the gardens there is delightful countryside with footpaths leading off the lane. When the woodland ends there are extensive views to the right and Crich Tower may be seen ahead through the trees. This is a monument to men of the Sherwood Foresters who died in the World Wars and an eternal flame burns at the top of the lighthouse-like tower. **At a T-junction turn right into Upper Holloway, descending a steep hill to meet a main road. Turn left and as you turn you may see a house named Lea Hurst ahead which was once the home of Florence Nightingale.** Go through the hamlet of Wakebridge to reach Crich where the entrance to the National Tramway Museum is to the left. Just before this you will see the former façade of the Derby Assembly Rooms, the work of Robert Adam, close to the road. The building was destroyed by fire but the front was salvaged and re-erected here.

Continue through the village on the main road past the beautiful Norman and fourteenth-century church to meet the B5035 and turn left to Alfreton. Keep on this road and you will soon see the dramatic outline of Wingfield Manor on the skyline. The drive to the historic ruin is on the right and 1/2 mile further on you come to the village itself.

A causeway leads out of South Wingfield village and the thirteenth-century church is just beyond a little bridge. **When you reach the B6013 at the Butcher's Arms pub turn right towards Belper.** There is soon another fine view of the ruins of South Wingfield Manor from the

Matlock Bath

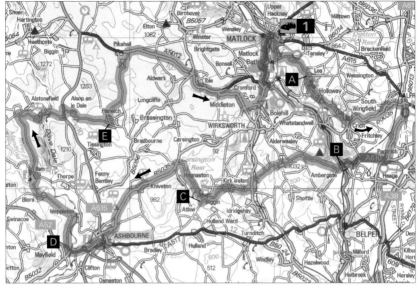

eastern side of the Amber valley with Crich Tower beyond. **At the A610 turn right towards Matlock.** Pass the turn to Belper on the left and keep on the main road for another 2 miles to pass through a place named Sawmill and meet the A6 at Ambergate. **Turn left towards Derby and then almost immediately right B before a chapel following the sign towards a youth hostel and crossing the River**

Derwent. The road climbs steeply with woods to the right. Keep on the main road when a byway leaves to the left. The quiet country lane wanders between stone walls past Wiggonlea and Netherpark farms. The tracks opposite both farms are rights of way giving access to the National Trust's Shining Cliff Woods.

At a major road cross straight over into Sandhall Lane heading for Alport and

Ashleyhay. At a second crossroads cross over again heading towards the radio masts on Alport Height. Shortly after this bear right down Back Lane towards Alport. There are far-reaching views from this road and an enormous quarry can be seen on the other side of the valley. **At the next crossroads (where the Alport Height car park is to the left) go straight on to**

• PLACES OF INTEREST •

Heights of Abraham Country Park & Caverns, Matlock Bath
Cable cars take visitors up from Matlock Bath to a 60-acre park which contains nature trails, a natural cave, and a lead mine worked in the sixteenth century. Open daily Easter to end of October, 10–5. Telephone: (01629) 582365.

Gulliver's Kingdom Theme Park, Temple Walk, Matlock Bath
A family theme park with log flume, a ride into an old lead mine and more conventional fairground attractions. Open daily April–September, 10.30–5.30 and weekends September and October. Telephone: (01629) 57100.

Peak District Mining Museum, Matlock Bath
Situated in The Pavilion at Matlock Bath, the museum illustrates 2500 years of lead mining in Derbyshire with the opportunity of visiting the adjacent Temple Mine. Open daily all year except Christmas Day, 11–4 (later in summer). Telephone: (01629) 583834.

Peak Rail, Riverside Station, Matlock
1996 should see the opening of another 1½ miles of track taking the line from Matlock to Northwood and making a 7-mile round trip for steam trains. Until 1968 this was part of the Midland Railway linking Matlock with Buxton. Peak Rail aim to restore

this line completely and run trains to Buxton again. Matlock Riverside Station is the southern terminus and headquarters of the railway. Trains run at weekends May–August with midweek services in June, July and August. Telephone: (01629) 580381.

Riber Castle Wildlife Park
The grounds of romantic Riber Castle give wonderful views over the Derwent Valley and contain a unique collection of wildlife featuring many rare and endangered species. The Riber lynxes are world-famous and some have been returned to the wild in their native habitats. Open daily (except Christmas Day) from 10. Telephone: (01629) 582073.

15

National Tramway Museum, Crich

cross the major road. At 1,034 feet (315m) this is almost the highest point of the Low Peak, an outlier to the south of the Peak District proper.

The road, signposted to Ashleyhay and Idridgehay, is unreasonably deemed to be unsuitable for motor vehicles after the crossroads. It drops down and Spout Lane joins it from the left. **Bear left when another lane joins from right and turn left again to Idridgehay when the road divides.** This is Barnsley Lane, a pleasant country byway which has hedges rather than stone walls. At the bottom of the valley it joins the B5023. Turn left to Duffield.

After ¹/₄ mile take the first turning right (Wood Lane) signposted to Kirk Ireton and Callow. Keep on the main road to Kirk Ireton, bearing left on to Hob Lane, a name which may recall the activities of a hobgoblin long ago. At Kirk Ireton the little church has a low, battlemented tower. **Keep on the main road through the delightful village heading for Callow and Hopton to come to a junction where the main road bends to the right at the village pump. Take the left turn here to Blackwall and** Hulland down Blackwall Lane. Occasional breaks in the hedges give views over a lovely landscape.

Keep ahead at a junction along Gibfield Lane to come to a main road and turn right C towards Wirksworth and Matlock. There is parking on the right for Carsington Reservoir, Britain's newest reservoir. The road then runs below the earth wall of the dam, a grassy slope with a footpath on top. At the end of the dam there is a Visitors' Centre which has exhibitions, shops, water sports, cycle hire and a restaurant. **At the B5035 turn left towards Ashbourne.** The road passes a turn on the left to Hognaston (only), and it is worth detouring down this lane to the beautiful village with its ancient church which has a remarkable carved Norman tympanum above the door. After this turning go through Kniveton –

where the little church is to the left of the road. Ashbourne can soon be seen ahead as the road descends.

Fork left to follow roadsigns towards the town centre of Ashbourne. There are gardens to the left as the road bears left to enter a one-way system following an 'All through traffic' sign. The town's main car park is to the right after this. **Turn right at traffic lights and then go straight over the following traffic lights following signs to Stoke and Leek (A52). Within about 200 yards turn right off this road, still following the sign to Leek, to come to Church Street. Turn left and pass Ashbourne church on the left. This road leads to a roundabout where you take the second exit, the A52 to Leek.** At Mayfield the A52 crosses the River Dove, and the Uttoxeter road (B5032) leaves to the left. **As you climb the hill after this junction take the little road on the right D signposted to Okeover, Mappleton and Ilam.** This turning is by an old tollhouse.

The lane leads through beautiful parkland with ancient oak trees. The Georgian Okeover Hall and picturesque medieval church with its ivy-covered tower are seen to the left. **When you leave the park turn left towards Blore. Just beyond Blore Hall turn right at a crossroads to Ilam and Dove Dale. Blore Pastures car park is to the right and overlooks Ilam and Dove Dale. Cross the bridge at Ilam and pass the monument which reflects the style of an Eleanor Cross.** It was put up by Jesse Watts Russell, who rebuilt Ilam Hall in the nineteenth century, in memory of his wife. **Go through the village, bearing right past the entrance to the country park (see page 21) and then follow the main road to the right at the next junction towards Wetton and Alstonefield.**

The road climbs to reach tiny Stanshope where the lane is lined with daffodils in the spring. **At a T-junction about 1 mile from Stanshope turn right to Alstonefield and Hartington. After 200 yards turn right again to Milldale and Ashbourne.** The lane leads past the car park at Milldale into the village. **Turn left to follow the river up the lovely dale and then turn right at the main road to cross the bridge over the River Dove. As you climb the hill turn left on to a lane to follow a sign to a car park.** The lane takes you to the A515 opposite the Alsop en le Dale picnic site and car park. **Turn left on to the main road and then, after ½ mile, turn right to head for Alsop en le Dale and Parwich.**

Pass the medieval church at Alsop en le Dale to reach Parwich. **At a T-junction in the village E where the church is to the right turn left and then bear right towards Newhaven and Buxton and pass the fine eighteenth-century hall to the right.** Keep on the main road which twists and turns to climb a hill. **As you climb look for a narrow lane on the right signposted to Pikehall.** At the top there is a breathtaking panorama of pastures and interlinked stone walls. About a mile along this lane another road joins from Parwich. **Fork right just before a little railway bridge on a road signposted**

to a car park for the High Peak Trail (Minninglow).

At the A5012 turn right towards Cromford. Keep on the main road past the Hollybush Inn at Grangemill where the B5056 crosses the route. The road descends a very attractive wooded dale (Griffe Grange Valley). **About 2 miles after the Hollybush Inn turn right on to the B5023 to Middleton. Keep on this road which branches to the left immediately (the main road ahead goes to Rider Point and Wirksworth).** There are fine views to be seen as the B5023 climbs up to reach Middleton. **At the end of the village turn right at the crossroads by the Rising Sun inn on to the B5035 to reach the picnic site on Middleton Top.** This site is a popular access point for the High Peak Trail. Middleton Top Engine House still contains the working steam engine which was built in 1829 to haul wagons up the incline. There is also a Visitors' Centre and cycles may be hired from here. **Return to the crossroads at the Rising Sun and go straight ahead towards Matlock.** The National Stone Centre is to the right. **Turn left to Cromford on to the B5036 at the T-junction passing the picnic site at Black Rock on the right as you descend the slope of Cromford Hill. At Cromford the route meets the A6. Turn left to return to Matlock.** ■

Ilam Country Park

KEDLESTON, SUDBURY AND TUTBURY FROM ASHBOURNE

58 MILES – 2½ HOURS
START AND FINISH AT ASHBOURNE

Two of the grandest mansions in Derbyshire, a medieval castle, and a succession of beautiful villages form only a part of the attraction of this tour. The route crosses the three major rivers of Derbyshire – the Trent, Dove and Manifold – and it is interesting to compare their contrasting scenery. There is also the chance of seeing Britain's biggest crater, caused by accident during the Second World War.

Take the Derby road (A52 south) out of Ashbourne and after 6½ miles, as you enter Brailsford, **turn left to Mercaston and Hulland.** Follow the main road round to the right towards

Hulland as you leave Brailsford. **After about a mile turn right A at crossroads and follow a sharp right-hand bend on to the lane signposted to Mercaston and Mugginton.**

Keep on towards Mercaston at the next junction where a lane goes to the left to Mugginton and at the following one keep ahead to Kedleston. The earth here is

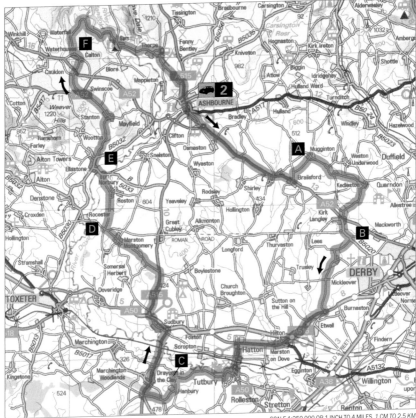

SCALE 1:250 000 OR 1 INCH TO 4 MILES *1 CM TO 2.5 KM*

Ashbourne

Situated at the point where the rolling pastures of south Derbyshire meet the harsher landscapes of the Peak District, the town has a justifiable claim to be the gateway to the Peak. It can also claim to have one of the finest churches in Derbyshire, dating from 1241 and having a spire 212 feet high. Many people visit the church just to see Thomas Banks's masterpiece, the statue of Penelope Boothby who died in 1793 at the age of five. It bears the inscription 'She was in form and intellect most exquisite. The unfortunate parents ventured their all on this frail Bark. And the wreck was total.' The monument is in the Boothby Chapel which also contains fifteenth- and sixteenth-century alabaster monuments of members of the Cockayne family. Note the beautiful gates at the eastern entrance to the churchyard. These were made by Robert Bakewell c. 1730.

Ashbourne is equally satisfying for its secular architecture. It has an abundance of almshouses dating from the seventeenth and eighteenth centuries, many of them situated in Church Street. The Grammar School, founded in 1585, is a prime the street and faces The Mansion, a grand town house which appears to be Georgian though the façade hides seventeenth- century work. Dr Johnson was very fond of Ashbourne and often stayed with his friend Dr John Taylor at The Mansion.

A bypass has recently taken a lot of traffic away from the town to rid its streets of much noise and fumes. Visitors will enjoy its variety of shops, many of them selling locally-made crafts. The Derwent Crystal factory shop adjoins Shaw Croft car park and you can see lead crystal being blown and decorated by craftsmen.

The annual game of football played through the streets each Shrove Tuesday attracts vast crowds who watch two teams attempting to take the ball from the middle of town over the Henmore Brook to mill races about 3 miles away from each other. There are only three rules to the game – there must be no murder or manslaughter, no use of vehicles, and if a goal has not been scored by midnight the ball must be given to the police.

Kedleston Hall

This is the most important Georgian house in Derbyshire, a grand Palladian mansion with a suite of rooms by Robert Adam which have survived almost without alteration since the house was built between 1759 and 1765. The rooms contain most of their original paintings and furniture and feature magnificent plasterwork by Joseph Rose. The house was built for Nathaniel Curzon, 1st Baron Scarsdale, so it is appropriate that visitors can see an Indian Museum which displays items collected by a later Lord Curzon when he was Viceroy of India. The 'Peacock Dress' worn by his wife at the Coronation Durbar in 1903 is in pride of place. The hall is surrounded by landscaped parkland with a serpentine lake which has a bridge and fishing pavilion also designed by Adam. Kedleston Hall is a National Trust property. Open April to October, Saturdays to Wednesdays 1–5.30. Telephone: (01332) 842191.

---

reddish, like that of Devon. Continue to head towards Kedleston, staying on the main road which dawdles along following the valley of the Cutler Brook to reach the village.

If you intend to visit Kedleston

Kedleston Hall

Hall you ignore a turn to the right which goes to Kirk Langley and go round a sharp corner to find the entrance to the hall to the right. **Otherwise the route continues by taking the turning to the right (Lodge Lane) to Kirk Langley. Turn left at a T-junction** – as you approach Kirk Langley the church can be seen to the right beyond a beautiful brick-built manor house. The lane meets the A52 at a crossroads. **Go straight over on to the B5020 to Mickleover.** After leaving the village go past Long Lane to the right and the Bluebell Inn on the left. The main road bends right and then left. **Take the turning to the right signposted to Radbourne on the left part of this bend by a South Derbyshire boundary sign.**

This is a good broad road through open countryside with a pleasant mixture of trees, cultivated fields and pastures. **Take the first turning left to Radbourne on a slightly more narrow lane.** The grand Georgian house on the hill to the left is Radburne (sic) Hall, the home of the Chandos-Pole family. **Turn right at the next junction to Dalbury and Etwall. Go straight over the crossroads which follows in about a mile.** Now the landscape is very flat. **At a roundabout on the A516 turn right towards Uttoxeter. Pass a turn to the right to Sutton-on-Hill and then turn left into Etwall, ignoring the following turn to the right to follow the main road into the village.** The elaborate gates of the Port Almshouses in the

The Port Almshouses and hall gates at Etwall

churchyard were made for Etwall Hall by Robert Bakewell of Derby c.1730. The hall was demolished in 1953 but the gates were rescued and re-erected in 1985.

Return to the main road and keep straight on at a roundabout to head for Hilton and Hatton on the A5132. Follow this road through Hilton to come to Hatton. **At the Salt Box Café turn left at the traffic lights on to the A50.** Cross the railway and then the River Dove to enter Staffordshire. The ruins of Tutbury Castle are seen to the right as you cross a second bridge. In 1320 a treasure

chest was lost in the river here by the Earl of Lancaster as he was being pursued by King Edward II. More than 500 years later, in 1831, the treasure was discovered by workmen digging gravel from the bed of the river. **Follow the sign ahead to Fauld at the roundabout on the edge of the small town. At Tutbury Mill Mews bear slightly to the right to leave the main road. Turn right into Castle Street at staggered crossroads at the end of this road (there is a car park to the left here) and climb the hill towards the castle to pass below its**

crumbling walls. Tutbury was an important stronghold of John of Gaunt and its oldest masonry (the remains of the chapel) dates from the twelfth century. However, most of what we see today is later, including the eighteenth-century Folly Keep which replaced a medieval one. The castle was besieged during the Civil War and left in ruins which, with the grounds, are open to the public.

Follow this road for about 2 miles past Fauld Quarry before turning turning left $\boxed{\text{C}}$ at the top of a hill following a sign to Hanbury. Just past the Cock Inn at Hanbury there is a footpath to the left of the road which leads to The Crater, the relic of an explosion at an underground munition dump in the Second World War which left the largest crater ever to be formed by conventional explosives. The footpath goes across fields to reach the remote site of the disaster and there is a touching monument to Italian prisoners of war who perished at the time which overlooks the vast scar in the countryside, a quarter of a mile wide.

• PLACES OF INTEREST •

Sudbury Hall
The National Trust handbook prints a warning that Sudbury's plasterwork and paintings can only be appreciated on bright days, and dull days in autumn should be avoided. There are also wood carvings by Edward Pierce and Grinling Gibbons, ceiling paintings by Louis Laguerre, and a richly-decorated staircase, to give the Sudbury interiors a rare splendour. The hall was built between 1661 and 1670 by George Vernon who employed many of the craftsmen who worked with Sir Christopher Wren on St Paul's and the City of London churches. The nineteenth-century service wing of the hall holds the National Trust's Museum of Childhood, containing items from many of their properties illustrating the lives of

children from the eighteenth century onwards. The Toybox Gallery has been specially designed to display a large collection of dolls and toys and there are even chimneys which today's young visitors may try to climb. Open April to October, Wednesdays to Sundays and Bank Holiday Mondays (but not Good Friday), 1–5.30. Telephone: (01283) 585305.

Norbury Church
The church stands next to the Manor House making an exceptionally picturesque scene in a wooded setting. Both buildings are of exceptional interest, the latter having a stone-built Norman hall (National Trust, open by appointment only). The church is more accessible and is well worth

visiting for its great east window with magnificent medieval glass which throws subtle light on the alabaster figures in the chancel. These date from the fifteenth century and are pioneering work of sculptors using alabaster from quarries at Chellaston and Tutbury.

Continue through the village after this and turn right at a junction to follow the sign to Newborough, Marchington and Uttoxeter. Hanbury church is down a cul-de-sac to the right. **Fork right when a road leaves to the left to Burton. Turn right on to the A515 to Ashbourne at a place appropriately called Six Roads End.** There is a fine view as you descend the hill into Draycott in the Clay. Cross the river to return to Derbyshire and **turn left to Sudbury just before reaching a roundabout.** Sudbury Hall is to the left before the loop road meets the A50. If you wish to visit the hall please use the car park on the right-hand side of the road. **Turn right off the main road (A50) immediately after joining the dual carriageway on to the A515 following signs to Cubley and Ashbourne. After about 2 miles turn left to Marston Montgomery at the first staggered crossroads.**

A quiet lane leads past venerable Vernon's Oak (on the left as the road bends right – it probably marked the outer limit of the Sudbury estate) and reach Marston Montgomery in about 2 miles where the church with its quaint little tower is to the right. **Go through the village and approximately 1 mile further on bear left when you meet a main road and then take the next turn right**  **to Roston and Norbury.** The rambling country lane leads into Roston. **Keep on the main road to Norbury where you join the B5033.**

If you wish to visit the beautiful church turn right here, otherwise **turn left to cross two bridges and re-enter Staffordshire to come to Ellastone. Turn right on to the B5032 to Mayfield and Ashbourne.** At the end of the village, after a lane on the left signposted to Leek leading past the church, **take the next left**

Throwley Hall

turn , **a lane signposted to Stanton.** This descends into the bottom of a lovely little dale with a stream. It corkscrews and then climbs steeply to give splendid views. At Stanton keep on the main road through the village heading for Cheadle and Leek. **At a major road (A52) cross straight over** on to a byway which gives more delightful views of the surrounding hills. **Go straight over the next major road (A523) to Calton and over the crossroads which follows after about a mile** and head towards Throwley and Ilam. **Turn right at the next junction** **on to a gated lane** again signposted to Throwley and Ilam.

There is a fine view as the road dips down after Throwley Moor to pass Throwley Hall, a ruined sixteenth-century mansion standing at the bottom of the valley next to a farmhouse and a pond. After the farmyard and gate here the lane can be seen

wandering through the meadows for a long way ahead. Note the signs of medieval cultivation here – ridges and furrows known as strip linchets. The lane eventually reaches a beautiful bridge over the River Manifold. **About a mile after this go right at a T-junction into Ilam.** The entrance to the Country Park is to the right. **Bear left by the elaborate memorial cross to Dove Dale and Thorpe.**

The turning to Dove Dale, a dead-end leading to a car park, is to the left after about a mile, and then the road climbs up to reach Thorpe where there is a short-term car park and toilets. Continue through Thorpe to reach the Dog and Partridge inn. **Follow the main road round to the right here towards Ashbourne. The road descends to cross a little bridge and then reaches the main road (A515); turn right to return to Ashbourne.** ■

The monument to Penelope Boothby, Ashbourne church

CHESTERFIELD, CRESWELL CRAGS AND HARDWICK HALL

52 MILES - 2½ HOURS
START AND FINISH AT CHESTERFIELD

Chesterfield may not be a glamorous town but many facets of its long history are interesting and these are illustrated both in the remarkable parish church and in the town's excellent museum. The surrounding countryside has a variety of landscapes, from lonely moor to snug valleys which could belong to Somerset or Devon. Two of the major architectural treasures of Derbyshire are visited in this tour – Hardwick Hall and Bolsover Castle – while Creswell Crags provides an insight into the way of life of the county's earliest human inhabitants.

The tour starts at St Mary's church, Chesterfield, whose famous twisted spire makes an unmistakable landmark. **Come down St Mary's Gate with the church to the right, to reach the roundabout at the bottom. Take the first exit here, the**

A61 to Sheffield, turning left before a bridge to join the dual carriageway. Keep on the A61 over a roundabout where the Worksop road, A619, goes to the right. At the second roundabout take the turning to the right to Eckington,

B6052, and pass beneath a railway bridge. About 1 mile after the roundabout, and just 3 miles from Chesterfield, you come to Whittington where the Revolution House is on the left by the Cock and Magpie Inn. The plaque on its wall reads:

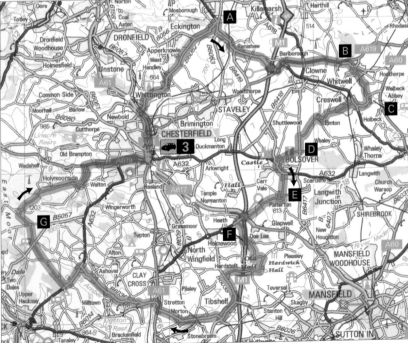

SCALE 1:250 000 OR 1 INCH TO 4 MILES 1 CM TO 2.5 KM

Chesterfield

As its name implies, the town had its origins in Roman times and grew steadily to be given a market charter by King John in 1204. It continued to expand throughout medieval times but rapid growth only occurred in the nineteenth century when the nearby coalfield generated heavy industry. George Stephenson lived at Chesterfield after building the Midland Railway through the town and is buried in Holy Trinity church.

Most people will know Chesterfield for the twisted spire of its parish church (St Mary and All Saints) which is 228 feet high and leans outwards 8½ feet on the south side. A legend has it that the Devil once paused for a rest on

one of his flights, and clung to the spire for a moment or two. However, incense drifted up from below and caused him to sneeze so violently that the spire twisted out of shape. More prosaically, the true reason for the warping is that the framework was built from unseasoned timber and distorted as it dried out. Although the church was restored in the nineteenth century most of it dates from the fourteenth. Numerous chapels, fine monuments and furnishings speak for the

prosperity of the town at this time.

Chesterfield remains famous for its market and official market days are Mondays, Fridays and Saturdays with a flea-market being held on Thursdays. Its shops also attract visitors from near and far, the town centre having undergone a successful face-lift.

Chesterfield Museum and Art Gallery, St Mary's Gate. Situated close to the parish church it is apt that the museum should have the medieval windlass used in the construction of the church together with other items showing the development of the town through the ages. The art gallery is notable for featuring the work of Joseph Syddall (1864–1942) who lived at Old Whittington. Open daily except Wednesdays and Sundays, 10–4. Telephone: (01246) 559727.

The Revolution House, Old Whittington. The picturesque cottage was once an alehouse called the Cock and Pynot (a local name for a magpie). In 1688 three noblemen met there to lay plans for the revolution which eventually brought William of Orange and Queen Mary to the throne. It is now a museum with period furniture, a video on the revolution, and exhibitions on local topics. Open daily Easter–October and at Christmas, 10–4. Telephone: (01246) 559727.

Cresswell Crags, Crags Lane on B6042 1 mile east of Creswell village. The caves in this limestone gorge situated near the Nottinghamshire boundary provide a fascinating insight into the life of man ten thousand and more years ago. The archaeological finds have been so important that Creswell has given its name to a specific Palaeolithic culture. Cresswellian man carved bone and one of the world's earliest works of art is an

engraved representation of a horse found in Robin Hood's Cave. Cresswell Crags is at the hub of a region embracing the former coalfields which, it is hoped, will achieve World Heritage status early in the next century. A Visitors' Centre has displays illustrating the way of life of Palaeolithic hunters and there are trails and footpaths of varying length which allow visitors to explore the area thoroughly. Visitors' Centre open daily February–October; Sundays only November–January, 10.30–4.30. Telephone: (01909) 720378.

Bolsover Castle. Although the Normans built a stronghold on this site overlooking the Vale of Scarsdale, the amazing ruin that we see today owes nothing to the militiary architect. At the heart of the vast hilltop complex is the keep designed by Robert Smythson in 1612 for Sir Charles Cavendish. The latter was Bess of Hardwick's favourite son, and he seems to have had a romantic streak which gave him a liking for the Arthurian style. Thus the 'Little Castle', his country retreat, has a host of romantic medieval features mixed with Italianate ideas derived from Inigo Jones. English Heritage have done wonderful work in restoring the decor to its original appearance. Sir William Cavendish continued building at Bolsover after his father's death in 1617. He put up the palatial mansion along the ridge to the south which has stood roofless since 1751 when material was taken from it to construct Welbeck Abbey. Fortunately the Riding School has survived and is still in use today, the disabled learning to ride in the grandest of settings. Open daily April–September 10–6. October–March, Wednesdays–Sundays, 10–4. Telephone: (01246) 823349.

AD1688. In a room which formerly existed at the end of this cottage, what is left of the old Cock and Pinnott, the Earl of Danby, the Earl of Devonshire,

and Mr John d'Arcy, the eldest son of the Earl of Holderness, met sometime in 1688 to concert measures which resulted in the revolution of that year.

Continue on the B6052 through pleasant countryside for about 3 miles to Eckington, **turning right when you meet the B6056 on the edge of the sprawling village.** The large

Cresswell Crags

church is unfortunately usually locked and is to the left almost at the bottom of the long hill leading to the village centre. **At traffic lights after the church** A **turn right on to the A616 towards the motorway (M1).** If you look to the left before you reach the bridge over the River Rother (which gives Rotherham its name) you will see Renishaw Hall on the skyline, its pinnacles and battlements unmistakable. The home of Sir Reresby Sitwell, its numerous ghosts include that of a boy in pink who is known as 'the kissing ghost' as he seems to enjoy doing this to guests. Renishaw is not currently open to the public.

Continue through Renishaw village. After 2 miles the road comes to junction 30 of the M1. **Keep ahead here on the A616, but at the next roundabout turn left on to the A619 following signs to Newark, Worksop, and the Rother Valley Country Park.** The road bypasses Barlborough, where the hall is an outstanding example of Elizabethan architecture and now serves as a preparatory school. **Keep ahead on the A619 over the third roundabout heading for Worksop.** The road crosses the A618 and ½ mile further on passes the Hotel Van Dyck (whose garden centre has a tea room). After this a road goes off to

Clowne to the right but **continue for another ½ mile and turn right** B **on to the Whitwell road (B6043).** The church at Whitwell dates from 1150 and the hall stands behind it. **Turn right opposite the church to Creswell down Scotland Street. Keep ahead at the following crossroads into Southfield Lane.** The road crosses a railway and passes the abandoned site of a coalmine. There is a quarry to the right. **Turn right just before reaching a bridge spanning the road to pass the Redland building materials works** (this unsignposted turning looks more like a factory entrance than a public road). **Turn right at a T-junction into Creswell.** Within half a mile you reach the car park for Creswell Crags C – 'the home of prehistoric man' – on the left.

Continue along the road which runs past the lake and the crags. **At the A616 turn right then take the turning left after ¼ mile to Creswell Colliery and Elmton.** The distinctive houses and cottages of the Model Village (1896–1900) are to the left as you drive through Creswell. Keep on the main road which climbs out of the village to reach Elmton. Follow the main road through the village. The church here is Georgian. **At a T-junction turn left on to the B6417 towards Bolsover. After just less than a mile turn right at the next**

crossroads D (this turn lacks a sign for this direction at the moment). In Bolsover you come to a junction where you face the church. In spite of suffering damage from fire on two occasions this is a fine building, notable for Cavendish monuments which the inscriptions claim to be humble but which in fact are massively ornate. **Keep ahead over the crossroads to pass the church, and then turn right to reach the castle.**

From the castle return to pass the church again and turn right on to the A632 towards Cuckney. After about ½ mile take the second turning right (**Mansfield Road**) to Palterton and in another mile or so take the **second** E **of the three turnings on the right to Palterton and Glapwell** (this is a crossroads). **Turn right at a T-junction into the village street.** The main road swings round to the right at the end of the village. **Keep ahead here down Rylah Hill** (the street sign is hidden in the hedge on the left). You see the M1 ahead as the road drops down to junction 29. Cross the motorway and then **take the turning left to Clay Cross (A6175) following the sign to Hardwick Hall. After about ¼ mile turn left again to Stainsby and Hardwick Hall. A mile further on turn left for the third time** F **on to a road signposted to Ault Hucknall**

Bolsover Castle

24

and cross beneath the motorway. There is parking for Stainsby Mill on the left (this is a working watermill belonging to the National Trust dating from the eighteenth century). **The entrance to Hardwick Hall Country Park is immediately on the right after the mill.** The route follows the drive through the ancient park and the National Trust may make a small charge for this (refundable if you pay to visit the hall). The drive offers an excellent view of both the magnificent Tudor hall and its medieval predecessor and leaves the park to go past the Hardwick Inn.

If you do not wish to visit the hall, keep on the main road at **F** which is adjacent to the motorway and rejoins the route at the exit

from the park opposite the inn.

Turn right after the pub and then immediately left at the main road to head for Hardstoft and Tibshelf. Turn left at the T-junction by the pub in Hardstoft taking the B6039 towards Tibshelf. Turn right on to the B6014 to Morton at another T-junction into Tibshelf. The tower of the fine church can be seen at the end of the street and a road to Alfreton goes off to the left after a thatched cottage at the end of the village. **Keep straight on towards Morton.** The church here, with its pinnacled tower, is at the end of the village after the Sitwell Arms. The road soon meets the A61 at Stretton. **Turn right and then left on to the B6014 following the sign to Tansley.**

Bear right, keeping on the main road (B6036), when the Matlock road (B6014) goes off to the left.

A delightful stretch of countryside follows with tree-covered hills and valleys. There is a particularly beautiful scene as you come into Ashover with the little River Amber at the bottom of the valley. The church is beyond the village square to the right and is usually open. It is interesting for the colourful alabaster tomb of Thomas Babington who died in 1518 and for its tiny lead font made c.1200 with small figures representing the Apostles.

At the A632 turn left towards Matlock and ascend Slack Hill. Take the first turning right at the top of the hill to Danby Dale and Beeley (the sign is well hidden on the left). Care is needed here to make the turn on a three-carriageway stretch of road. This hilltop road gives fine views and after about 1/2 mile a lane to the right leads to a picnic place after 200 yards or so. **Cross straight over the B5057 following the sign to Beeley and Chatsworth.** There are now stone walls lining the road rather than the hedges seen during earlier parts of the drive.

When you come to a major road G turn left (but not acutely left) to continue on the road signposted to Beeley and Chatsworth. After about 1/2 mile leave this road by taking the first turning right on to a road lacking a signpost (the turn comes just before a weight restriction sign on the major road). Now keep on the main road which crosses Holy Moor – the heather-covered high ground which overlooks Chatsworth to the west and Chesterfield to the east. The latter is seen below as the straight road descends a long hill. **Go through Holymoorside and at a T-junction turn left to reach the A619. Turn right to reach Chesterfield town centre.** ■

• PLACES OF INTEREST •

Hardwick Hall
Bess of Hardwick must have been a formidable character. She had four husbands and outlived them all, increasing her wealth as each one died. She spent much of her fortune building great houses, two at Hardwick and one at Chatsworth. In 1568 Bess married for the last time, her husband being George Talbot, sixth Earl of Shrewsbury. At Hardwick she began by enlarging the original manor house which had been her birthplace but when the earl died in 1590 Bess began building anew, siting the new mansion next to the old and making it a prodigy of glass and stone, 'the most adventurous house to survive from the Elizabethan age.'

Although she probably had help from the architect Robert Smythson, the house seems to reflect Bess's unbending and energetic character. The state rooms are on the second floor and instead of battlements her initials 'E.S.' decorate the tops of the towers. The old lady was seventy when she began building the new hall, and her efforts ensured that it was completed in seven years. She was almost ninety when she died in 1608 but at Hardwick her spirit lives on. The house is a splendid monument to an indominatable character, though the thought persists that it must have been torture to live or work with her.

Hardwick Old Hall (English Heritage), open April–October, Wednesdays, Thursdays, Saturdays, Sundays and Bank Holidays 12–6 (but 10–4 in October).

Hardwick Hall (National Trust), open April–October, Wednesdays, Thursdays, Saturdays, Sundays and Bank Holidays 12.30–5 or sunset. Country Park open throughout the year, dawn to dusk. Telephone: (01246) 850340.

BUXTON, ARBOR LOW AND HADDON HALL

44 MILES – 2 HOURS
START AND FINISH AT BUXTON

This drive takes you through byways which show the upland landscape of the White Peak to best advantage. It also provides the opportunity of seeing villages like Youlgreave and Hartington, the mysterious stone circle of Arbor Low, and Haddon Hall, perhaps the most romantic of all stately homes.

Take the A53 out of Buxton to pass the Opera House and Pavilion Gardens on the left, heading for Leek. Stay on this road when the Congleton road leaves to the right as you leave the town. About 1½ miles after this junction take the road to the left **A** signposted to Dalehead. The road can be seen winding across the top of the hills for a long way ahead. This is rugged limestone countryside where quarrying is an important industry but nevertheless there are plenty of footpaths and places to park and picnic. **At a junction just after a cattle-grid turn right following an unofficial sign to**

Fough along a little unfenced road past the exposed limestone of High Edge. A lane to Fough goes off to the right but keep ahead to cross another cattle-grid. Tor Rock is the great spine of rock ahead but the road swings left away from this and begins to descend through steep-sided Dowel Dale. The spectacular Parkhouse Hill is on the left and Chrome (pronounced 'Croom') Hill on the right. The local name for the vista of the two hills is The Dragon's Back. Dowel Cave is on the right just before Dowall Hall and was used as a burial-site in Neolithic times, ten bodies being discovered there.

Turn left on to the B5053 towards Buxton to pass through Glutton with its one lovely farmhouse and climb through another little ravine. **At a crossroads turn right to Earl Sterndale.** The little village suffered bomb damage in the Second World War and its church was almost destroyed. The raiders were attempting to bomb the ammunition dumps concealed in quarries nearby. **Keep on the main road to pass through the village and towards the end**

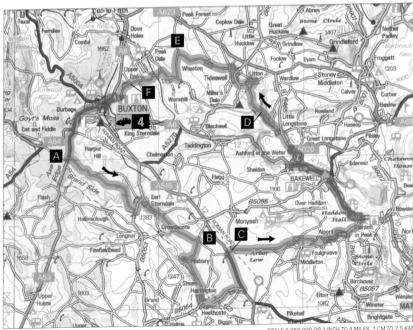

SCALE 1:250 000 OR 1 INCH TO 4 MILES *1 CM TO 2.5 KM*

turn left towards Pilsbury and Hartington.

The fine conical hill to the right is High Wheeldon which belongs to the National Trust. The road provides good views down to the right beyond railings as it twists round the hill. **At a major road go straight over, again following signs to Pilsbury and Hartington. Turn right at the next crossroads B to Pilsbury on to a gated road** (if you are not prepared to open the five gates on this lane ignore this

turn and continue along the main road to reach the A515 at Parsleyhay). There are fine views as you follow this winding byway which descends into upper Dove Dale after twisting through the farmyard at Pilsbury Grange. The next stretch is well used by ramblers but almost too soon it comes to Hartington, a picturesque village with a good choice of pubs and teashops. Pass the pond and turn left on to the main road opposite the Minton House Hotel. This is the B5054

which follows beautiful Hartington Dale to cross the Tissington Trail at which point there is a car park and picnic site.

At the A515 turn left for about 2 miles to come to a staggered crossroads. Here take the road on the right signposted to Youlgreave, Monyash and Arbor Low. After about 200 yards turn right C, now following the sign to Youlgreave, Lathkill Dale and Arbor Low. Drive for another 1/2 mile and then look to the

---

• PLACES OF INTEREST •

Buxton Spa

The Romans came to Buxton in the first century AD, saw the sparkling warm water with its distinctive bluish hue flowing from the foot of St Ann's Cliff, and established a small village close by. Naturally, an important feature was the spa baths, unfortunately overbuilt when The Crescent was put up in the eighteenth century. In medieval times the medicinal qualities of Buxton's mineral-rich waters were rediscovered, and the springs were dedicated to St Ann, the patron saint of cripples. In the sixteenth century Buxton Old Hall was built 'for the convenience of bathers' and Mary Queen of Scots lodged there when she visited Buxton seeking a cure for her rheumatism in 1573. This was during the years when she was a prisoner under the

care of the Earl of Shrewsbury (husband of Bess of Hardwick). The Old Hall, the oldest of the spa buildings, was rebuilt in 1670 and is now put to use as a hotel. A century later the fifth Duke of Devonshire decided to develop Buxton as a spa town. He commissioned John Carr of York to build The Crescent, an elegant range of buildings which was designed to include a town house for the duke (at the centre – his coat of arms on the façade), two hotels, lodgings and shops. Stabling was essential for the eighteenth-century traveller and the duke next built a grand building for visitors' horses, at an appropriate distance from The Crescent in order to avoid noise and smells. The coming of the railway made the stables

unnecessary and since 1859 this has been the Devonshire Royal Hospital. The large circular exercise yard at its centre, originally open to the sky, is covered by a vast dome which, when it was erected in 1881, was the largest in the world. The spiritual needs of visitors were met with the building of a church immediately to the west of the stables. This was completed in 1811 in an Italianate style which contrasts with the Victorian mosaics and furniture found inside. The Victorian era saw the last stages of the development of the spa with the landscaping of the gardens, the building of the Pump Room opposite The Crescent, and a Concert Hall and Opera House close by to provide entertainment for residents and visitors alike.

right for a sign to Arbor Low.
Go up the farm track to a car park situated just before the farmyard. A small charge is made, payable at the farmhouse.

Turn right out of the track to continue the tour. A road to the White Peak (part of a Scenic Drive) goes off to the right. Keep on the main road. **At the next junction – just beyond a quarry – go straight on towards a picnic area.** The main road bends round to the right here towards Youlgreave. Bear right again when the road divides to pass the Moor Lane picnic site on the right. Continue along this quiet country lane enjoying the views over Lathkill Dale and (a little further on) Youlgreave. **Fork left when you get to this village and then immediately turn left again at a major road.** Pass the church and drive down the main street – as at Hartington a range of refreshments are available in Youlgreave.

The road drops down sharply into Lathkill Dale and soon reaches Alport, a place of beautiful streamside cottages which was once a lead-mining centre. **At a road junction keep on the main road (B5056) towards Bakewell.** There are

more lovely views of the stream running through meadows at the bottom of the dale. **At the A6 turn left towards Buxton.** The car park for Haddon Hall is to the left within ½ mile of this junction. **At Bakewell keep on the A6 through the town, bearing left at the roundabout by the Rutland Arms hotel.**

Ashford in the Water is 1½ miles from Bakewell. **Turn right off the main road on to the A6020 towards Chesterfield and Sheffield. Almost immediately turn left off this road into the village, following the B6465 to Monsal Head and Wardlow. The next turn also follows at once – turn right opposite the Ashford Hotel on to the road to Monsal Head (B6465).** Continue on this road to Monsal Head, a celebrated beauty spot where the main car park is to the left, and there is a tearoom and pub. **Turn left off the main road after the car park to Upper Dale and Cressbrook.** There is a classic view of the dale and the disused railway viaduct as you descend. **Bear left to keep to the road which runs along the bottom of the dale** to pass the car park at Upper Dale and reach the ruined mill at

Cressbrook. Orphaned children used to work at cotton spinning here in the nineteenth century and endured much cruel treatment. Richard Arkwright built the first mill in 1783 but this only lasted for two years before burning down. At that time there was also a peppermint mill in the dale which used the wild mint growing in the woods. **By the mill fork left D to climb a 1 in 5 gradient on an unsignposted road which joins with a major road at the top just beyond a 'Victorian Garden'.** There is a spectacular view to the left as you head for Litton, keeping on the main road. **At a T-junction in the village turn left to follow the main road to Tideswell and Miller's Dale.** Litton has lovely stone cottages and a fine green with stocks and a pub but its church only dates from the 1920s. **When you reach the B6049 turn right to Tideswell. Drive into the centre of the little town up the broad main street, but just before the church with its remarkable pinnacles fork left to follow the sign to Wheston.** The road passes a little market square. **About 100 yards after this branch left up a lane still following the sign to**

Hartington

Wheston. Go through this small hamlet and descend down a steep winding dale to Dale Head, where there is a choice of footpaths, northwards up Haydale or south to follow the Limestone Way through Monk's Dale to Miller's Dale. The latter takes you through a National Nature Reserve. There is roadside parking a little further on when the lane broadens. **At a T-junction E turn left towards Wormhill and after about a mile at the following junction turn right towards Tunstead and Peak Dale.** A turn to the left is a cul-de-sac going to Tunstead and Chee Dale which can form part of a fine circular walk through Chee Dale returning via Wormhill. James Brindley, the self-taught genius who did more than anyone to build England's network of canals in the eighteenth century, was born in a cottage at Tunstead in 1716. Keep on the main road heading for Buxton to pass a vast cement works on the left. After a quarry the main road bears right and is signposted to Buxton. **However, carry straight on at this point F on a lesser road prohibited to goods vehicles.** This leads past the golf course on Fairfield Common and then meets the A6 on the outskirts of Buxton. **Bear left here to return to the town centre past a succession of Victorian houses.** ▪

• PLACES OF INTEREST •

Arbor Low

Known locally as 'The Stonehenge of the Peak', this is one of the largest stone circles in England and dates from c. 2000 BC. There are 47 stones today, none of them still standing upright. The stones were originally enclosed by a henge – a roughly circular area surrounded by a ditch cut from the rock and a bank. In the Bronze Age, when the circle was in use as a ritual site, woodland covered the hills so that those attending would not have been able to see the lovely vistas that can be enjoyed from here today. Just to the west of Arbor Low is Gib Hill where there is a large barrow (burial mound) dating from the early Bronze Age. The hill takes its name from a local murderer whose remains hung in a gibbet here in the eighteenth century.

Haddon Hall

Experts are divided as to whether Haddon is a mansion or a castle, Pevsner describing it as the English castle *par excellence*. However it is described it remains one of the most beautiful and romantic of buildings, occupying a matchless site overlooking the River Derwent from a well-timbered hillside. The earliest masonry dates from the twelfth century but most of what we see is

either fifteenth-century or Tudor, the south front containing the long gallery having been added in 1600. Haddon came to the Vernon family in 1170 and they kept it until Dorothy Vernon eloped with John Manners in 1558. It has been the seat of the Manners family ever since, and this occupation by one family (earls and later dukes of Rutland) is one reason why the house has managed to maintain the

atmosphere of the Middle Ages into the present time. The other reason for this preservation is that Haddon was unoccupied between 1740 and 1912. Miraculously, walls and roofs remained intact with the passing years, and the subsequent restoration was successful in retaining the original character of the house. Open daily April–September (but closed on Sundays in July and August) 11–5. Telephone: (01629) 812855.

BUXTON, MILLER'S DALE AND CHATSWORTH

45 MILES – 2 HOURS
START AND FINISH AT BUXTON

Put aside a whole day for this tour if you intend to visit Chatsworth en route. Just to view it in its incomparable setting is an experience, but seeing its rooms and the treasures they contain takes you into a different world. The tour also includes Tideswell, Youlgreave and Eyam, the latter a village with a tragic past, and there are miles of glorious countryside in between.

Tideswell church

Take the A6 eastwards out of Buxton going towards Matlock. The road follows Ashwood Dale and then Wye Dale with the river close to the left. After about 3 miles Wyedale car park is to the left opposite a cement works. The car park is useful to walkers exploring footpaths in Wyedale or those going through Deep Dale on the south side of the A6. A little further on there are views to the left towards Chee Dale and one of the largest of Derbyshire's quarries. The main road climbs out of Wyedale and at the top of the hill the A5270 leaves to the right to Brierlow Bar. **Keep on the A6 for another ¼ mile** and then turn left to take the B6049 to Miller's Dale and Tideswell **A**. This road descends into Miller's Dale with its spectacular crags. The Miller's Dale car park is reached by taking the road to Wormhill and crossing the bridge on the left. Pass underneath the railway viaduct now used by the Monsal Trail. After this the road passes a youth hostel on the right and about ½ mile further on enters Tideswell Dale where there is a picnic site to the right.

Stay on the B6049 through Tideswell, passing the lovely church known as 'the cathedral of the Dales', to reach the A623. **Turn right and then left by the**

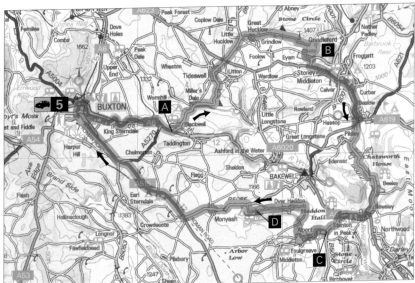

SCALE 1:250 000 OR 1 INCH TO 4 MILES *1 CM TO 2.5 KM*

Anchor pub keeping on the B6049 to Bradwell and Great Hucklow. The road is straight for about 2 miles. **When it bends turn right to follow a sign to Great Hucklow Gliding Club.** Go over a crossroads which follows immediately and into Great Hucklow. Drive straight through the village towards Bretton. The road gradually climbs up to the top of Hucklow Edge giving grand views on both sides. **Bear left when you meet a major road coming up from Foolow.** After the Barrel Inn the road swings to the right while a track goes ahead to the radio mast at the summit of Sir William Hill. After this the road begins to descend. A footpath on the right drops straight down to Eyam. **At a main road turn right ▣ to**

Eyam Hall

Eyam. There is a steep drop to the left as the road descends. Pass the car park to come to the centre of the village. **Turn left into the main street** – the car park for

Eyam Hall is to the right. The church comes immediately after the hall; both are to the left of the road. **About ¼ mile after the church take the first turn**

· *PLACES OF INTEREST* ·

Miller's Dale

John Ruskin wrote that you might have seen the Gods in this dale before it was despoiled by a railway running through it. The railway closed long ago, but tastes have changed and today people enjoy walking along the old line and most are pleased that it was 'enterprised through the valley' against Ruskin's wishes. The dale took its name from the old corn mill here which was worked by the power of the River Wye.

Tideswell

With a population of about two thousand, Tideswell hovers between being a village and a town. Tideswellians can justifiably lay claim to its being a town, pointing out that it gained its market charter in 1250. The wonderful church was built in the comparatively brief time of 75 years beginning about 1320, most of its benefactors having made fortunes from lead mining or the woollen trade. It contains some outstanding pre-Reformation monuments and brasses – one of the best of the latter commemorates Bishop Pursglove who died in 1579. In spite of this

post-Reformation date he is shown wearing the eucharistic robes of a High Church supporter of the Pope. Tideswell's remote location fostered its own traditions. Oat cakes were a staple part of the diet in bygone times and are still baked here. Local morris men perform a dance unique to the town at the well-dressing and there is a famous tradition of music-making.

Eyam – the Plague Village

In many respects the village has similar origins to Tideswell – its early prosperity was based on lead-mining and wool, though this seems to have come earlier than at Tideswell for Eyam church dates from the thirteenth century and was rebuilt in 1618. Disaster struck the village in September 1665 when a tailor, who lodged at a cottage by the church, received a roll of cloth from London. It arrived damp and was opened out to dry. This released fleas which carried the plague bacilli and within a few days days the tailor, his landlady and one of her sons had died. Neighbours died soon afterwards and within a month fearful inhabitants were beginning to leave Eyam. Realising the

danger of the plague being spread throughout the countryside the rector, William Mompesson managed to persuade the villagers to isolate themselves. Food and other supplies were left at the parish boundaries and church services performed in the open air at Cucklet Delf where the Plague Commemoration Service is still held each year. Mompesson's wife was one of 259 victims who died at Eyam before the plague ended a year later (about two-thirds of the total population). Plaques on some of the cottages are tokens of tragedies of the two-year epidemic and many people come to Eyam drawn by the story. However, this is one of the most attractive of Derbyshire villages and there is much more to see than reminders of the events of 1665–66. There is a fine ninth-century Saxon cross in the churchyard while Eyam Hall dates from 1676, a beautiful manor house which has been the home of the Wright family for more than 300 years.

Eyam Hall open April–October, Wednesdays, Thursdays, Sundays and Bank Holiday Mondays and Tuesdays, 11–4.30. Telephone: (01433) 631976.

The waterfall in Lathkill Dale

Chatsworth House

It is easy to put aside a day to visit Chatsworth, 'the Palace of the Peak', and come away with the feeling that it would take several more visits to appreciate all of its multitude of treasures. These do not belong solely to the house – the grounds provide equal fascination. While everyone knows the Maze and the Emperor Fountain, it is easy to miss the romantic Aqueduct hidden in woodland beyond the little summerhouse at the top of the Cascade. The earls of Devonshire were rich and powerful even before the fourth Earl lent his support to deposing James II from the throne and replacing him with William of Orange and his wife, Queen Mary. The fourth Earl's ancestor, Bess of Hardwick, had put up a large Tudor house on the site, the first of her many building projects. When William of Orange rewarded the fourth Earl with a dukedom he felt that this house inadequately reflected his new status. At first he set about enlarging the earlier house, but as work progressed he became more ambitious and by 1707 it had been engulfed by the new building, a symmetrical mansion with a pleasing unity of style. The foremost artists and craftsmen of the day were hired to decorate its rooms. The grounds also reflected the taste of the time and The Canal Cascade was constructed following the principles laid down by Le Nôtre. In the mid-eighteenth century the fourth Duke employed James Paine to improve the parkland surrounding the house and he engineered the sweeping approach road and the beautiful bridge over the River Wye. It was the sixth Duke, who came to the title in 1811 with family fortunes enhanced by their flourishing copper and lead mines in the county, who enlarged the comparatively compact seventeenth-century house into a vast palace by adding a north wing in the 'Picturesque' style fashionable at the time. He promoted Joseph Paxton to the post of head gardener, and Paxton, a genius typical of the age, designed the Emperor Fountain which shoots water to a height of 290 feet as well as a Conservatory (now demolished) which served as a model for his tour de force – the Crystal Palace he built for the Great Exhibition of 1851. Visitors to Chatsworth see an almost unrivalled display of magnificence, the contents of the house enhanced by items from Chiswick House and Devonshire House, the family's former London residences.

House and gardens open Easter–October, daily 11–4.30.

Farmyard and Adventure Playground open Easter–September, daily 10.30–4.30. Telephone: (01246) 582204.

Caudwell's Mill

The mill was built by John Caudwell in 1874 and harnesses the water of the River Wye to drive original machinery to mill flour by the roller method. Visitors can see the mill in operation on the second Sunday in each month but at other times can simply admire the intricate Victorian machinery. Craft workshops include those of a glass blower, potter, and wood turner and there is also a riverside Nature Trail.

Open daily March–October 10–6. Weekends only November–February 10–4.30. Telephone: (01629) 734374.

right to Bakewell and then turn right again on to a major road to descend the hill (if you miss the first turn carry on for 150 yards and turn right on to the major road).

When this road meets the A623 turn left towards Baslow and Chesterfield. Go through Stoney Middleton and straight over traffic lights at Calver to remain on the A623. The road crosses the River Derwent and then follows it into Baslow. Pass the little church and take the second exit (A619) at a roundabout towards Bakewell and Chatsworth. Keep straight on towards Matlock on the B6012 (the major road) when the A619 goes off to the right to Bakewell. Stay on the main road when the B6048 joins from the right. The road enters Chatsworth Park and passes Edensor village to the right. The driveway to Chatsworth House is on the left.

The B6012 leaves the park over a cattle-grid and there is a car park and picnic site immediately after this on the right,

just before the bridge. After crossing the River Derwent again the road passes Beeley. Like Edensor, this is a village belonging to the Chatsworth estate. At Rowsley you come to the A6. Turn right towards Buxton. Caudwell's Mill, a Victorian flour mill still worked by water-power, is to the left with its complex of craft workshops. At the end of a short stretch of dual carriageway turn left on to the B5056 to Ashbourne. After about a mile turn right at the first junction **C** to Youlgreave, staying on the major road. The road climbs up the lower part of Lathkill Dale to reach Alport and then Youlgreave.

Opposite Youlgreave church turn right to Over Haddon. Turn right again at a T-junction and cross Conksbury Bridge, a favourite place to start walks up Lathkill Dale. There is a steep drive xup from the bridge with a few parking places by the side of the road. Take the first turning left after about a mile, still heading for Over Haddon. At

Over Haddon bear left to join a major road which leads into the village and then take the first right to Haddon Grove and Monyash. This turn is by the Lathkill Dale Craft Centre. Pass a lane leading to a car park to the left as you leave the village. A mile from Over Haddon turn left when the road divides to Haddon Grove. Halfway along this lane **D** you can park near a farm driveway on the left which is part of a right of way leading down to Lathkill Dale, one of the loveliest of all the dales with its woods and waterfall. Continue along the lane to come to the B5055, where you turn left to Monyash. The approach to the village is puzzling – you see its picturesque buildings on top of a hill ahead but then the road dips down and you lose sight of them before it climbs again to reach it. Monyash has a tearoom, pub, lovely church, and countless stone cottages. After driving straight through the village you come to the A515 in about a mile. Turn right to drive the 7 miles back to Buxton. ▪

Miller's Dale

WIRKSWORTH AND DOVE DALE FROM DERBY

START AND FINISH AT DERBY
53 MILES – 2½ HOURS

This tour strikes northwards from Derby and passes through attractive countryside to reach Wirksworth, a fascinating little town too often neglected by visitors. From here the way lies westwards to Dove Dale and Ilam where you turn to head back on quiet lanes through a succession of interesting villages.

Leave Derby city centre heading northwards for **Matlock on the A6** and pass Allestree Park on the left before coming to Duffield. **Pass the post office here and turn left just before the Midland Bank on to a lane (King Street)** which is signposted to Hazelwood. **After the New Inn bear left to keep on the major road towards Hazelwood and Shottlegate.** The pleasant country lane comes to the A517. **Go left and then right to cross it on to Lamb House Lane**

heading for Shottle. After this village the landscape gradually becomes more rugged and stone walls replace hedges. Keep on the main road following signs to Alderwasley, Ashleyhay and Alport heading directly towards radio masts on the top of the hill. Stay on the major road when a road goes off to Ashleyhay on the left, bearing right towards Wirksworth and Breamfield along Alport Lane. A National Trust car park **A** (Alport Height) is at the top of the hill on the right by the radio masts and, at 1,034 feet, is an excellent viewpoint. The Alport Stone is a gritstone monolith standing just below the car park which has been a training-ground for rock climbers for several generations.

Keep on Alport Lane, the main road, over crossroads. There are magnificent views as the road runs high on the flank of the hill and suddenly Wirksworth comes into view below. **When you reach the B5035 turn left to drop down into Wirksworth.**

Turn left at the main street and then immediately right following Heritage Centre

---

• PLACES OF INTEREST •

Dove Dale
The most famous beauty-spot in the Derbyshire Dales, Dove Dale struggles to survive the impact of many thousands of visitors on its delicate landscape. Izaak Walton laid the foundations of the popularity of Dove Dale when he published the first edition of *The Compleat Angler* in 1653. Walton shared the writing of the second part of the book with Charles Cotton. The idyllic picture they painted of Dove Dale and adjoining Beresford Dale (where Cotton was squire) appealed not only to anglers but also attracted artists and writers, among them J.M.W. Turner, Byron, Dr Johnson and John Ruskin. Today Dove Dale is almost too famous and on the busiest days 3,000 people an hour have been counted walking the 2½ miles between the stepping-stones and Milldale. This means

that there may be 6,000 people on the footpath at these times. The National Trust owns most of Dove Dale and has done its utmost to maintain the path in good condition. Inevitably in this century it has broadened from being a narrow path wandering by the river to a mini-highway easily walkable at all times of year. The Trust has also removed many sycamores which grew up in the last hundred or so years and obscured spectacular limestone features such as Tissington Spires. Eroded slopes have been planted with rowan, hazel and blackthorn and the river re-stocked with trout and grayling. On Thorpe Cloud areas have been fenced off to allow the grasses to re-generate. It is thought that it will take five or more years for the ground to recover. It is to be hoped that all the effort will preserve this wonderful

landscape so that it can be enjoyed just as much by future visitors.

Tissington Trail
This is part of the old Buxton to Ashbourne railway which was closed in 1967 having operated since 1894. A typical country branch line, it took milk to London from farms in the dales, stone from quarries, and provided a local passenger service. The National Park bought 11 miles of the line in 1968 and re-surfaced the trackbed to make it ideal for walking or cycling. This trail, with the High Peak Trail which the Tissington Trail joins at Parsley Hay, has become a major tourist attraction and motorists can park at many points to take to feet or bike-saddle to enjoy the wonderful scenery away from busy roads. Cycles may be hired at Parsley Hay. Telephone: (01298) 84493.

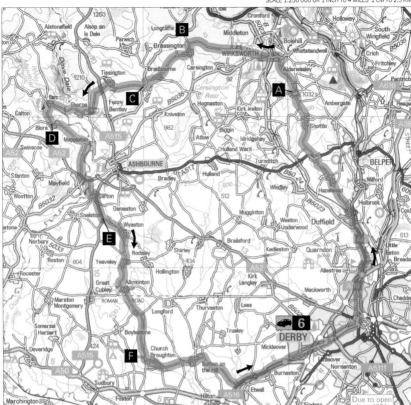

signs to pass a town-centre car park to the left. **Climb the steep hill and take the first major turning right to Brassington and Longcliffe.** The road continues to climb steadily. **At a main road (the B5035) turn right and then left, still heading to Brassington.** There is a long straight stretch of road with the embankment of the former railway which is now the High Peak Trail close to the right. Note the limestone formations to the right just before a cement works (Longcliffe quarries). This is a popular rock-climbing ground. **At a T-junction B turn left to Brassington, Kniveton and Ashbourne.**

In the middle of Brassington turn right to Bradbourne and Ballidon. In the days of the stage-coach the village was important, for this was where the turnpike road from Derby and London ended.

Travellers had to use rough cart tracks across the limestone hills to reach Buxton and Manchester. This is why Brassington once had nearly a dozen inns and alehouses though only two survive today. **Turn right again by the Miner's Arms pub to pass the Norman church and the post office. Once out of the village bear left when the road**

divides to head for Bradbourne.

At Bradbourne the church is half-hidden to the right at the centre of the village. There are remnants of Saxon masonry in the north wall of the nave. From Bradbourne head for Fenny Bentley and Ashbourne, enjoying the splendid scenery of this part of the drive. **Descend to the**

Tissington

35

Okeover Hall

B5056 and turn left to Ashbourne. Take the first turning right **C** after ¹/₄ mile on to an unsignposted road which crosses a beautiful, gravel-bottomed ford. After this the road crosses open meadows to reach Tissington (the Tissington Trail which follows the old railway line between Ashbourne and Buxton is reached from the information centre and picnic site passed on the left as you enter the village).

Tissington is a showpiece village which has belonged to the Fitzherbert family since the seventeenth century. Pass the pond on the left and a road leading to the church and Jacobean hall to the right and enter Tissington Park. The ridges and furrows made by early farmers are well seen here – they may date from Saxon times when the land was cultivated by teams of oxen. At the end of the parkland go over a cattle-grid and through a gateway to reach the A515. **Cross straight over to Thorpe and Dove Dale.** There is a car park and picnic site on the left just before the Dog and Partridge inn. **Turn right by the pub to join the major road heading for Thorpe, Dove Dale and Ilam.** Thorpe Cloud, a grass-covered conical hill, is an obvious landmark as the road drops down into Thorpe village. Pass through Thorpe – there is a short-term car park and toilets

near the end of the village. Farmers open up fields for car parking in the vicinity during busy times in the summer and a popular footpath leads down to Dove Dale from the village. The road is unfenced as it descends through pastures with Dove Dale to the right.

The lane to the main car park for Dove Dale is to the right by the entrance to the Izaak Walton Hotel. The route continues ahead to Ilam. **Turn left here to cross the bridge, heading for Blore,** but if you wish to visit Ilam Country Park turn right. The road climbs out of the village and there are fine views looking back. At the top of the hill, after the road crosses a cattle-grid, there is a picnic place with a fine view (Blore Pastures). A little further on Blore church will be seen across a meadow to the right. **At the crossroads by the church D turn left to Mapleton** (on this signpost but with two 'p's on the map) and Ashbourne.

The pleasant country lane descends and leads past beautiful parkland. The imposing portals of Okeover Hall will be seen to the right just before a bridge. **Take the turning right into the park after the portals but before the bridge following the sign to Mayfield.** There is a lovely view of the Georgian hall with the tiny, ivy-covered church close by as you begin driving through the park (where no parking is

allowed). The stable block is some distance to the right. Some of the oak trees in the park are very ancient. Leave the park over a cattle-grid and, after about ¹/₂ mile, you will come to a T-junction. **Turn left on to the A52.** At Mayfield pass the Queen's Arms and the Uttoxeter road (B5032) on the right and cross a bridge over the River Dove to pass the Royal Oak on the left. **200 yards after a filling station take the turn to the right to Clifton (the village shop is on this corner).**

The road crosses the valley and passes an old railway house, easily recognisable even though there is now no trace of a railway line. The road climbs up through a rocky ravine to come to a T-junction beside a church. **Turn left following the sign to Ashbourne, and then turn right at the next junction on to the A515.**

At the end of a stretch of three-carriageway road climbing a long hill turn left E to Edlaston and Wyaston. Pass Edlaston Hall on the right and then, after another ¹/₂ mile, the church on the same side. **At a T-junction by the Shire Horse inn turn right into Wyaston and keep on the main road through the village.**

Yeaveley is the next village. **At a junction by its brick church bear right on to a major road.** The village was the birthplace of one of the most famous medieval mason-architects, Henry Yevele, who worked at Westminster Abbey and Canterbury cathedrals in the fourteenth century. Keep on the main road to Alkmonton where the church is on the lane to the left. From here the quiet rural byway with hedges on either side and very little traffic leads to Church Broughton. Keep on the main road when a road to Boylestone goes off to the right and you will reach Church Broughton after about 2¹/₂ miles. **At a crossroads F turn left into the village to pass the**

Derby

The Cathedral. The splendid early sixteenth-century tower of the cathedral, 212 feet high, dominates the city's skyline but gives a false impression of the church itself. This was rebuilt 1723–25 to designs by James Gibbs who broadly followed the principles he had already executed at St Martin's-in-the-Fields. It was the parish church of Derby until 1927 when it was given cathedral status. Between 1968 and 1972 the cathedral was extended eastwards when the retrochoir, baldacchino, sacristy, etc were added. The beautiful wrought-iron screen which divides the nave from the chancel was executed by Robert Bakewell of Derby and was the work that established his reputation. Remarkably there are many fascinating monuments which pre-date the rebuilding. The Cavendish Area, which was St Katharine's Quire or Chapel in the medieval church, contains the enormous tomb of Bess of Hardwick. Her alabaster effigy was completed six years before she died in 1607. This was the burial-place of the Cavendish family until 1848. The cathedral is as full of beauty and interest as many of its medieval counterparts (and is more colourful than most).

Derby Museum and Art Gallery, The Strand. The museum reflects the fascinating history of the city over the ages and there are excellent examples of early Derby porcelain, etc. Predictably there are many paintings by Joseph Wright of Derby (1734–97) in the Art Gallery. His use of light dramatically enhanced his portraits and allegorical works and greatly influenced later artists. Both Museum and Gallery also stage temporary exhibitions. Open all year, Tuesdays–Saturdays 10–5, Mondays 11–5, and Sundays and Bank Holidays 2–5. Telephone: (01332) 255586.

Royal Crown Derby Factory, Osmaston Road. Derby was one of the earliest places where porcelain was manufactured, the first pieces dating from c.1740. The Crown Derby factory has examples of porcelain from this time onwards and displays also illustrate the intricate details of production. Visitors can also see craftspeople at work decorating modern pieces. Open weekdays 10–12.30 and 1.30–4 (except during factory holidays). Also Guided Tours. Telephone: (01332) 712800.

Pickford's House, 42 Friar Gate. The house was built in 1770 by Joseph Pickford, a prominent architect of the day, and its rooms illustrate domestic life of the period. There is also a costume exhibition and cooking and laundry demonstrations in which children can take part. Open Mondays 11–5, Tuesdays–Saturdays 10–5, and Sundays and Bank Holidays 2–5.

Derby Industrial Museum is on the site of the silk mill put up by John Lombe in 1717 on the River Derwent opposite the cathedral. The dramatic story of John Lombe is told here. He stole secrets of Italian silkmaking and is supposed to have been poisoned by the Italians when they realised his deceit. Later developments are also illustrated, most notably the continuing saga of Rolls-Royce where sound effects enhance stories such as that of the Merlin engine which powered the Spitfire. Open Mondays 11–5, Tuesdays–Saturdays 10–5, and Sundays and Bank Holidays 2–5. Telephone: (01332) 255308.

---

church which has a squat tower topped with a tiny steeple.

Much of Church Broughton belonged to the Duke of Devonshire until the early years of the twentieth century. The Duke found the villagers so boisterous that he had one of the first police houses in Britain built here in 1855 – appropriately it is still called Peel House. Keep straight on through the village heading for Sutton, Hatton and Longford along a twisty lane. **Keep ahead towards Sutton and Longford at the first junction.** The countryside is very flat now. **At a major road cross straight over heading for Sutton on the Hill. When you come to a T-junction turn right to Hilton and then after 100 yards left to Trusley and Etwall** to pass a battlemented Gothic hall on the left – this is Sutton Hall which was built to serve as the vicarage c.1820.

The next junction is Devil's Elbow – turn right towards Etwall and pass the drive to Ashe Hall School. At the A516 turn left to Derby (or right if you wish to visit Etwall village first). The final part of the route bypasses Mickleover to return to Derby. ∎

St Helens, Derby

REPTON, CALKE ABBEY AND THE VALE OF TRENT FROM DERBY

START AND FINISH AT DERBY
55 MILES – 2½ HOURS

The tour passes through countryside very different from the highland scenery of most of the other drives. It will do much to dispel the notion that there is little of interest south of Derby. Repton and Melbourne are both charming small towns with outstanding churches while Calke Abbey, Elvaston Castle and Staunton Harold are places where man-made beauty mingles with historic interest.

Leave Derby on the A514 signposted to Melbourne and Swadlincote. This road passes the Derbyshire Royal Infirmary on the left and the Crown Derby Factory on the right to come to the new relief road at Osmaston (2½ miles from the city centre) and then passes through Chellaston before crossing the new southern bypass. After this the road goes over the railway and then the canal. Note the strange-looking building in the middle of a field to the left at Swarkestone. Known as the Summer House, it overlooks a small enclosure where bull-baiting and similar sports probably took place and thus served as a kind of grandstand. It dates from c.1631. Swarkestone church has alabaster tombs of the Harpurs who inhabited the Hall before it was demolished after the Civil War and the family moved to Calke Abbey.

Keep on the A514, turning left to cross the medieval bridge over the River Trent after the junction with the

A5132. Turn right immediately after the bridge  **A to Ingleby and Foremark.** There are picnic places by the river which are popular with anglers and a lake made from abandoned gravel workings is to the left. About 2 miles along this lane, just after the hamlet of

Ingleby, there is a tricky crossroads on a steep rise where the main road bends left. **Turn right here to Foremark and Milton.** The enormous cooling-towers of a power station are ahead. A charming little gate-lodge to Foremark Hall on the left guards an imposing gateway. The Palladian hall was built in 1759 for Sir Robert Burdett, M.P. and houses the Repton Preparatory School. The ironwork of the gates is almost certainly the work of Robert Bakewell of Derby. Footpaths leave from the opposite side of the road to a cave on the bank of the River Trent which was once an anchorite's cell (an anchorite was a religious hermit). **At the Coach House inn at Milton turn right at a T-junction to Repton.** At Repton follow the main road towards the centre of the town at first. **However, the route bears left away from the town centre when the road divides by the Boot Inn, to follow signs to Swadlincote and Bretby and come to the High Street. Turn left here.**

The way out of the town is a pleasant country road following a small river to the left lined by willows and ash trees. **About a mile after leaving Repton turn left B at a junction by a**

Calke Abbey

beautiful little lake and cross a bridge giving a view of a waterfall, following the sign to Bretby, Hartshorne and Swadlincote. There is a parking place here for walks over Repton Common to Foremark Reservoir.

The road climbs and gives fine views over the Vale of Trent on a good day. **Turn right at a T-junction on to Ticknall Road.** The road heads towards the embankment on the shore of Foremark Reservoir. The first entrance to the reservoir is reserved for anglers and sailors. However, the next entrance is open to the public and gives access to car-parking for picnic areas and walks.

Continue on the road skirting the reservoir to reach the A514 at Ticknall and turn left. The B5006 goes to the right – take this road if you wish to continue the route without seeing Ticknall or Calke Abbey, otherwise continue into the centre of the village. There is a small car park to the left after the fine-looking Victorian church with its tall spire.

Until 1981 Ticknall belonged to the Harpur-Crewes of Calke Abbey who charged a peppercorn rent for the village's beautiful cottages but in return expected service from the villagers in

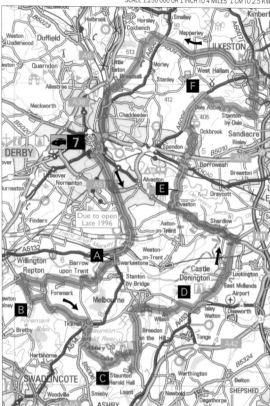

almost feudal style. The little conical building on the main street served as the village lock-up until the First World War and was designed so that anyone placed inside was unable to lie down comfortably. Since there were eight alehouses in the village in Victorian times the lock-up often had an occupant, though Mrs Soar who lived nearby, had a key and could be persuaded to release the prisoner for a consideration. If you wish to visit

Elvaston Castle

Calke Abbey turn right just before the bridge at the end of the village.

Having explored Ticknall **return down the main street and turn left to Ashby-de-la-Zouch on the B5006. After about a mile turn left to Staunton Harold (there is a picturesque lap-boarded bus shelter by this junction).** The lane runs through very pleasant countryside notable for its mature oak trees. **At a major road** C **turn left to Calke and Staunton Harold.** Just beyond the Saracen's Head pub there is a driveway to Staunton Harold church (National Trust) which may be used by the public except at busy times such as Bank Holidays or Sundays in summer when a one-way system is operated (see below). At these times access is from the B587. However, the mile-long drive through the park makes a very pleasant way of visiting Staunton Harold. The church belongs to the National Trust and is almost unique in being built during Cromwell's rule, by Sir Robert Shirley who was an ardent supporter of the King. Its interior retains many of the original furnishings. There are tearooms at the garden centre and at Staunton Harold Hall which belongs to the Sue Ryder Foundation (not open). The Ferrers arts and craft centre is situated opposite the garden centre. **After visiting Staunton Harold continue down the**

drive and cross a bridge to reach the B587. Turn left to Melbourne.

If you do not wish to drive through the park or you are following the route when the one-way system is in force keep on the lane which turns sharply right in Calke village. It then crosses a bridge over an arm of the Staunton Harold reservoir and there is a car park to the right. **Turn left on to the B587 towards Melbourne** (or right to visit Staunton Harold at busy times). There is another parking place and picnic area by the reservoir on the left as you come to the town.

Turn right by the market cross in the middle of Melbourne to pass the parish church, the hall and the lake. Then follow the road by the estate wall into Wilson. The church on the top of the hill to the right is that of Breedon on the Hill. **Turn left as you come to Wilson to head for Castle Donington and Isley Walton.** You are now in Leicestershire. **Turn right at the next junction** D **by Park Farmhouse Hotel to continue to head for Castle Donington.** The motor racing circuit faces you at this point. **Turn left when you meet the A453 in Isley Walton and then left again on to the un-numbered road to Castle Donington and pass the entrance to Donington Park on the left.**

Castle Donington has a

delightful mixture of old buildings. Many of them are built from the from the stonework of the castle which commanded the town from its hilltop site in Norman times. The thirteenth-century church and the town centre are to the right of the main road. **Continue on the B6540 through the town and at traffic lights turn left on to the A6 towards Derby.** Cross the River Trent again and pass Shardlow Marina on the right by the Navigation Inn (see Tour 20). **2 miles after Shardlow turn right on the B5010 to Borrowash.** Drive through Thulston and after about ½ mile the entrance to Elvaston Castle Country Park is on the left E.

After this the road crosses the River Derwent to reach Borrowash and the A6005. **Go left and then right across this main road to head for Ockbrook.** Borrowash had both a railway and a canal until the 1960s when the railway was taken up and the canal filled in.

A bridge takes you over the A52 and into Ockbrook. The village church is to the right of the road and was rebuilt in 1803. It has three fine monuments by Westmacott. A Moravian settlement (one of only three of the strict order in the country) was founded in the village in 1750 and comprises a fine group of houses with adjoining chapel. It is to the left of the route through Ockbrook. In the nineteenth century the village produced luxury goods, silk gloves and fine stockings – Queen Victoria's stockings came from Ockbrook.

Turn left at a T-junction to head for Ilkeston and reach the A6096. Turn right on to the main road following the sign to Ilkeston and Kirk Hallam. After nearly 2 miles turn right opposite a nursery F **to Dale Abbey.** The remains of the abbey are to the right of the road and are reached by one of the innumerable footpaths which criss-cross this lovely district.

Dale Abbey

Follow the main road as it twists round and take the first main turning to the left to Stanton-by-Dale. At a main road bear left to come into the village past the Stanhope Arms pub and the beautiful village pump. This is Littlewell Lane which descends into the industrial outskirts of Ilkeston. At the next main road (Low's Lane) turn left towards Kirk Hallam and Ilkeston and then immediately right on the road signposted to Little Hallam. This road takes you to a roundabout on the outskirts of Ilkeston. Turn right here on to the A6096 and follow the main road round to the left heading for the town centre and Nottingham. Keep on the main road and climb a hill before turning left on to the A609 towards Belper at a roundabout.

After about 4 miles on the A609 cross straight over the A608 heading for Woodside and Horsley. At the next

Derby Cathedral

junction, where the main road bends sharply right, turn left to Morley and Brackley Gate up Cloves Hill. After climbing the hill take the first turn left to Morley and Breadsall up Quarry Road. Keep on the main road to approach Derby through pleasant countryside. Pass Breadsall Priory Hotel on the right. This was the home of Erasmus Darwin, poet, physician and philosopher who died there in 1802.

The church at Breadsall has one of the finest medieval spires in the county. This fortunately survived the fire started by suffragettes in 1914 which severely damaged the interior. Pass the church and the post office and continue along the road through the village to turn right on to Croft Lane. This takes you to a roundabout where you turn left to follow the A61 and then the A52 back to Derby. ■

• PLACES OF INTEREST •

Repton
The parish church is dedicated to St Wystan, who was murdered in 849 and was buried here with his forefathers, three of them kings of Mercia. Wystan's remains became greatly venerated and it seems likely that the incomparable Anglo-Saxon crypt of the church was built as a shrine. Unfortunately, King Cnut disinterred St Wystan in the eleventh century and carried his bones to Evesham where they continued to attract pilgrims until the Reformation. The Anglo-Saxon parts of the church (of which the crypt is the most important) are, in the words of Pevsner, 'one of the most precious survivals of Anglo-Saxon architecture in England.' Most of the rest of the church is medieval, the tower and spire dating from 1340 and rising to a height of 212 feet, exactly the same height as the tower of Derby cathedral. The church originally stood next to a large Augustinian priory whose buildings were taken over by Repton School on its foundation by Sir John Port in 1557. Many of the monastic buildings are still used by the school.

Calke Abbey
'The house that time forgot' came to the National Trust in the 1980s, a great baroque mansion which stands in the middle of parkland well timbered with oak trees as old as the house. Because of declining fortunes and a succession of bachelors, the Harpur-Crewe family left the mansion cocooned in the Victorian era. Sir Vauncey Harpur-Crewe, who died in 1924, was the last member of the family to marry and when he did so in 1876 he simply abandoned the room he had grown up in to move to more suitable quarters. Thus on acquiring the property the National Trust found this room just as he had left it. Other rooms remained as they were on Sir Vauncey's death. He disapproved of motor cars, which visitors had to leave outside the gates. If they were fortunate he sent a landau to take them the 2 miles to the house. This dates from 1703 and was built on the site of an Augustinian priory by Sir John Harpur who had tired of his previous home at Swarkestone. The Abbey is well worth seeing for its architectural splendour, but its recent history gives it unique appeal. Open April–October, Saturdays to Wednesdays 1–5.30. Telephone: (01332) 863822.
Donington Collection of Grand Prix Racing Cars, Donington Park. World's largest public display of Grand Prix cars and racing motor-cycles. Open daily except Christmas and New Year's Day, 10–5. Telephone: (01332) 810048/812919.

41

LYME PARK AND
PEAK FOREST FROM BUXTON

START AND FINISH AT BUXTON
45 MILES - 2 HOURS

The tour takes you into Cheshire to see Lyme Park where a Palladian façade hides Tudor interiors. At New Mills you are back in Derbyshire to wonder at the way the cotton industry developed and then declined. The route skirts Hayfield and Chapel-en-le-Frith to pass through Sparrowpit and Peak Forest – the latter being renowned as a place where clandestine marriages could be performed. There are many opportunities to stretch your legs, not least towards the end of the drive at Miller's Dale.

Take the A53 out of Buxton (the Leek and Congleton road) past the Pavilion Gardens – a pleasant green way out of town. **Pass the snow indicator boards and bear right to Congleton and Macclesfield on the A54 when the trunk road divides.** You are soon on the wild moors with the road climbing steadily. **After another 1½ miles follow the main road to Macclesfield**

(A537) round to the right when the A54 leaves to the left. From here you can see the Cat and Fiddle inn on the skyline ahead. A road to the right goes to Derbyshire Bridge only (where there is a picnic site and car park). You enter Cheshire about a mile before the Cat and Fiddle inn. Standing at 1,690 feet it is England's second highest inn after the Tan Hill above Swaledale. The Cat and Fiddle is just 5 miles from

Buxton and was built to allow the changing of horses after the hard climb.

There are wonderful views from the road which, perhaps because of this, has more than its share of accidents. **2¾ miles after the Cat and Fiddle turn right at a crossroads A to Saltersford and the Goyt Valley.** The road drops down steeply and there is a good view of Lamaload reservoir ahead. At the end of the reservoir a car park and picnic place serve a network of footpaths allowing a fine choice of walks. About ¼ mile beyond the car park the road divides. **Turn right B to follow a sign to Saltersford, Kettleshulme and the Goyt Valley.**

However, those with a liking for mysteries may like to walk up the road to the left for about 150 yards. A stone on the left side of the road is a memorial to John Turner, 'cast away' at this spot in a snowstorm in 1755. The mystery comes from the inscription on the reverse: 'The print of a woman's shoe was found by his side in the snow where he lay.'

The road twists and turns through the dale to reach the very remote St John's church, Saltersford (the Jenkin

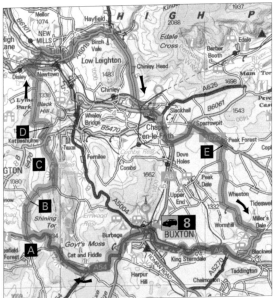

SCALE 1:250 000 OR 1 INCH TO 4 MILES *1 CM TO 2.5 KM*

Chapel). The unusual building was consecrated in 1733 and takes its name from a Welsh drover who often passed this way and may well have preached here. Although it is usually locked you can obtain a good impression of the unspoilt interior with its box pews by peering in at the windows. Saltersford's name reflects its being on one of the Saltways made for packhorses carrying salt from the Cheshire mines.

Keep on the main road which bears right and climbs steeply from the chapel. At the top of the hill there is a wide parking area. **Turn left at the following junction to Kettleshulme and Whaley Bridge.** The Plym Chair car park is immediately on the right and gives splendid views. Footpaths lead into Goyt Forest. The road winds down to an upthrust crag

The Jenkin Chapel

ahead, the Windgather Rocks, which are favoured as a practice ground by rock-climbers. Soon after this you reach a crossroads **C** where the road to the left goes to Dunge Farm Gardens.

At **C** keep ahead to Kettleshulme which proves to be a lovely little village. Turn

right on to the B5470 to pass the school, the Bull's Head, and Ye Swan. On the far side of the village, as the 30 mph limit ends, turn left down Kishfield Lane. About ½ mile down the pretty lane turn left at an unsignposted junction **D** to leave the major road as

The Cage, Lyme Park – a Tudor hunting tower

and bridges – including the modern one which takes the main road away from Chapel-en-le-Frith. **Having passed beneath this bridge turn left at a roundabout following signs to Buxton (A6). At a second roundabout turn right on to the A6 and after 1½ miles leave this main road at the next roundabout, taking the first exit, the A623 to Sparrowpit, Peak Forest and Castleton.**

At the Wanted Inn turn right towards Chesterfield, continuing to follow the main road. The Wanted Inn was known as the Devonshire Arms for almost four centuries. However, in 1956 the Duke sold his Peak Forest properties and the pub was put up for sale. It remained on the market for two years, and in that time it became known as 'the pub which nobody wanted', so that when the inn eventually re-opened it was named the Wanted Inn. Sparrowpit may take its name from the fluorspar pits which are still worked here.

An enormous quarry can be seen to the left which takes up much of a hillside. **At Peak Forest turn right 🅴 to Smalldale and Wormhill.** Now the landscape has made a subtle change and is much more rolling and open with little stock in the fields, most of them growing grass for silage. There is none of the cragginess seen earlier yet very few trees either. **Keep ahead when the main road swings**

this swings right. The lane descends steeply to a small bridge and climbs equally steeply up the other side. It is narrow, the corners are blind and so is one of the summits. **At a T-junction turn right.** The road climbs steadily towards the Moorside Hotel. Lyme Park is to the left and you can see The Cage, a Tudor watch-tower from which deer could be spotted. The lakes in the park can also be seen.

At a T-junction turn left to Disley on to Buxton Old Road and descend into the village. At traffic lights turn left if you wish to visit Lyme Park, otherwise turn right on to the narrow road (A6).

Pass the Dandy Cock pub and take the next turning left down Redhouse Lane. Cross the canal and descend by the railway line to come to another T-junction where you turn right to negotiate a hairpin bend and cross the River Goyt. On the right is Torrs Riverside Park and Hague Picnic Site – a waymarked walk starts from here and links with the Sett Valley trail, a long-distance footpath which runs from Manchester to Hayfield. **Turn right when you reach a main road (B6101).** There is a view across the valley to the vast Torr Vale and Rock mills opposite. **At a mini-roundabout turn right –** the New Mills Heritage Centre is

immediately to the right. **Cross the River Goyt again and then turn left at traffic lights on to the A6015 to Hayfield.** This road takes you across the River Goyt for the third time. There are fine hills to the left as the road comes to Birch Vale. After this there is another interlude of countryside before the road comes to Hayfield. **Join the A624 by turning right at a T-junction to Chapel-en-le-Frith** but turn left off this main road almost immediately if you wish to see Hayfield village.

There is magnificent dales scenery to be seen from the stretch of the A624 beyond Hayfield. About 3½ miles from the village the road passes beneath a bridge and comes to a T-junction. **Turn left to keep on to the A624** and come to Chapel Milton where there is a complicated system of viaducts

Hayfield

right, about 1 mile from High Peak (at the moment there is no signpost here). Go past a turn to the left to Wheston and at a T-junction turn left to Wormhill and Miller's Dale. Wormhill is a much more appealing village than its name might suggest. The parish church is off to the left, a Victorian building incorporating hardly anything of the previous medieval church. It is dedicated to St Margaret, famous for her expertise in slaying dragons and serpents. The name of the village suggests a connection with one of these monsters.

The lane out of the village is frothy with cow parsley in early summer and the scenery becomes

The former station at Miller's Dale on the Monsal Trail

much more typical of the dales with many more trees. The crags of Miller's Dale appear ahead and the road dips down into the dale to go below the old railway – Miller's Dale car park is to the

right just before the bridge. **Turn right on to the B6049 following the sign to Buxton and when this road meets the A6 turn right again to return to Buxton.** ■

• PLACES OF INTEREST •

New Mills

In the mid-eighteenth century the first mill was built in the valley of the River Sett. At this time the township of New Mills did not exist. It only came into being in 1884, the new parish incorporating a number of small hamlets strung along the valleys of the rivers Sett and Goyt. The first of the mills was built for grinding corn but later cotton mills spread here from Lancashire and the two narrow valleys became crowded with industry. The Torrs is the name given to the gorge of the River Goyt which has been made into a country park. New Mills also has an excellent Heritage Centre illustrating the history of the district, both before and after industrialisation.

New Mills Heritage Centre, Rock Mill Lane. Open Tuesdays–Fridays 11–4, Saturdays and Sundays 10.30–4.30 (4 in winter). Telephone: (0663) 746904.

Lyme Park

The great house was given to the National Trust in 1946 by Richard Legh, third Lord Newton, whose family had owned the estate since 1388. The outward classical appearance of the mansion gives little hint that there is an

Elizabethan house within, but visitors will find themselves in a succession of rooms which seesaw between Tudor, Palladian and nineteenth-century styles. The furnishings of the rooms reflect all of these periods, with the Mortlake tapestries and Grinling Gibbons woodcarving outstanding. There is also a unique collection of English clocks. The gardens have a lake, an orangery by Lewis Wyatt, and a formal garden in 'Dutch' style. Beyond, there are nearly 1400 acres of parkland which are grazed by herds of red and fallow deer. The Cage is a tower built in Tudor times as a hunting tower (there is a similar one at Chatsworth). While it may have helped to spot where deer were grazing at the start of the hunt, its prime purpose was probably to allow ladies to enjoy watching the chase itself.

Open April–October, Saturdays to Wednesdays, 1.30–5 (11–5 on Bank Holidays). Park open daily 8–8.30 or dusk. Telephone: (01663) 762023 or 766492.

Peak Forest

The name of this tiny village seems completely misleading at first but in fact it derives from the Royal Forest of the Peak, an area of about 40 square miles created in

Norman times as a royal hunting-ground. Even then few trees grew on the hills but wild boar and deer abounded, as did wolves. A court used to meet here to make sure that the forest laws were not interpreted too harshly. The forest remained a royal game preserve for more than 500 years, the laws being revoked in 1674. The land then belonged to the earls of Devonshire and the original church was built in 1657 by the wife of the second earl. This was during the time when the Commonwealth had banned church building – to add insult to injury the countess dedicated it to King Charles the Martyr. Because of this unorthodox foundation the church did not belong to a diocese and the incumbent found that he could apply his own ecclesiastical rules. Thus it became known as 'the Gretna Green of the Peak'. Many eloping couples came to Peak Forest for an instant ceremony, and the vicar was able to supplement his income. The practice was ended in 1804 by Act of Parliament. The seventh duke built a new church on the site in 1876 and all that survives of the old one is a Venetian window, the original east window, incorporated in the Reading Room to the right of the new church.

· TOUR 9 ·

EDALE AND CASTLETON FROM BUXTON

37 MILES – 2 HOURS
START AND FINISH AT BUXTON

The scenery of Edale is justly famous but fewer people explore Errwood Reservoir with its poignant reminders of the great house which once stood here. You will probably like to spend some time in Castleton with its fascinating little shops, some specialising in Blue John, the rare form of fluorspar only to be found here, which is made into brooches and similar ornaments.

Take the A5004 to Whaley Bridge from Buxton, passing the Devonshire Hospital on the right. At this point it is signposted to 'Stockport via Long Hill'. The road climbs steadily up Long Hill to the moor. **After about 2 miles take a turning to the left A to the Goyt Valley which comes as the**

main road swings right just after a National Park sign.

There is a fine view of the main road to the right as it follows the contours below Hanging Rock. The road passes a little roadside shrine to Our Lady on the right, a reminder that the Errwood valley was a stronghold of Catholicism throughout the hundred years that

the Grimshawe family occupied the hall. After this the road descends past a little pond with the Goyts Lane car park close by. There is a splendid view ahead over the two reservoirs (Errwood and Fernilee) and you pass toilets and another car park before the road runs along the top of the dam between the reservoirs. Errwood Hall car park is to the left at the T-junction while The Street car park faces you. The Spanish Shrine in the grounds of the hall was built by family to the memory of a governess, Dolores, who died in 1889.

Turn right at the T-junction to Kettleshulme. The road

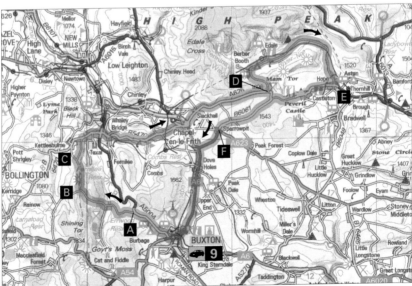

SCALE 1:250 000 OR 1 INCH TO 4 MILES *1 CM TO 2.5 KM*

• PLACES OF INTEREST •

Errwood Hall

The hall was built in 1830 by Samuel Grimshawe, the founder of the Catholic family which ruled over the Goyt valley for more than a century. He built the hall as a wedding present for his son and it became a notable estate, more than 20 people being employed there at the height of its prosperity. The Grimshawes had their own steam yacht and its captain must have been held in great affection as he is buried in the private graveyard above the hall. The family must have also loved Dolores, a Spanish governess, as they built her a charming little shrine hidden in the woods. Mary Gosslin, the grand-daughter of Samuel, was the last of the Grimshawes to live at Errwood. When she died in 1930 the estate was bought by the Stockport Corporation Water Undertaking and the hall pulled down. However, its foundations can still be seen, as can the graveyard and the poignant Spanish shrine.

Chapel-en-le-Frith

The name means 'Chapel in the Forest' after the chapel built in 1225 by the foresters of the Royal Forest of the Peak, the game preserve of Norman and medieval monarchs. The small community surrounding the chapel soon grew and a more commodious church replaced the chapel in the fourteenth century. However, it was not large enough to hold the 1500 men of the Scottish army kept captive there for nearly three weeks in 1648 by the Duke of Hamilton. 44 of them died of overcrowding in the church and more perished later on the forced march into Cheshire. By the eighteenth century, when the church was given a Georgian facelift, Chapel was a busy market town and administrative centre (later it became known as 'the Capital of the Peak'). The medieval town stocks are preserved in the market place which is covered with stalls on Thursdays, market day. The greatest boost to the town's fortunes came in 1897 when an amateur inventor, Herbert Frood, emerged from his garden shed with a brake block made from cloth impregnated with resin. Noting the difficulties suffered by carriers as they brought their wagons down the steep hills into the town, he saw that they coped most successfully if they fitted an old boot on their brakes. Thus he was able to call his invention a brake-shoe and establish the Ferodo factory in the town.

The Chestnut Centre

The conservation park takes its name from the chestnut tree standing by the entrance to the car park. The tree was planted to commemorate Queen Victoria's coronation in 1837. The Centre was founded in 1984 with the aim of promoting a wider understanding of our natural environment and is particularly successful in promoting the issue of conservation to schoolchildren. Specialisations of the Chestnut Centre are breeding programmes for otters and barn owls, and many of these threatened animals have been raised here to be successfully released into the wild. Buzzards, little owls, kestrels and badgers have also been bred at the Centre and set at liberty at suitable sites. Visitors are able to see many of these species in aviaries and enclosures. There is a large area of parkland for picnics (and also a café) as well as a nature trail and a shop. Open March to December daily, January and February weekends only, 10.30–5.30. Telephone: (01298) 8140.

climbs out of the Goyt Valley to the top of the moor. **At a junction by the Goyt Forest car park turn right** **to Kettleshulme and Whaley Bridge.** The road gives a splendid view with Windgather Rocks ahead – a popular training ground for rock climbers. Half a mile further on there are crossroads where you can go left to Dunge Farm Gardens (see page 43). **Turn right here** **to Whaley Bridge.** There are more fine views to the left from this narrow, twisty lane. Keep on the main road when a track goes off to the left at a fairly sharp right-hand corner. **At the main road (B5470) turn right** (the Toddbrook reservoir is to be seen ahead as you turn).

Go straight over at traffic lights to cross the A5004, keeping on the B5470 to Chapel-en-le-Frith. This is a very pleasant, quiet road (most traffic uses the dual carriageway which bypasses Chapel). Look for

a pub on the right called the Hanging Gate. This is at a hamlet named Tunstead where there was a famous ghost named Dickey who was so disruptive that he caused the railway to be diverted. Dickey's skull is supposed to rest in a farmhouse at Tunstead to this day in spite of many efforts to get rid of it.

Go through the town along its straight main street which is much quieter than it used to be when the main road ran through it. **Follow the signs to Buxton and Manchester (A6) but more importantly watch for those to the Chestnut Centre and Blue John Cave. Be careful not to join the bypass, having passed underneath it, but keep straight ahead to follow the sign to Rushup, Edale and the Chestnut Centre.** The latter is a conservation centre and is to the left about a mile beyond the bypass. After passing the Centre

there is a lovely view down to Ford Hall, a much-altered Jacobean house. The road follows quite a narrow dry valley, climbing gradually to reach Rushup Edge. There are good views to the right even though the landscape is scarred by a large quarry.

3 miles from Ford Hall look for a somewhat concealed turning to Barber Booth and Edale on the left **which comes when the road reaches a patch of woodland.** There is a picnic site on the main road just beyond the turning. Take this road to Edale which climbs steeply to pass below Mam Tor and then provides wonderful views as it zigzags down into Edale.

Edale is set in a natural amphitheatre. There are plenty of parking places where you can watch the toy-like trains pursuing their course through the Pennines. A track can be seen on the far side of the dale climbing steeply – this is the start of the Pennine Way going up to Jacob's Ladder. The descent into Edale makes ears pop if you go too quickly. A road to Upper Booth goes off to the left and Edale car park is just after the turn to 'Edale village only'.

A mile beyond the village the road crosses beneath the railway line – this marks the beginning of a fine scenic drive along the Vale of Edale. The trees on top of the ridge as the road begins to swing southwards are at the top of Woodlands Valley and will overlook Ladybower Reservoir. Win Hill is the summit at the southern end of the ridge. Eventually you come to the main road at Hope opposite the beautiful old church . **Turn right to Castleton on the A625.**

Castleton is famous for Peveril Castle, its old church, innumerable show-caves, and Blue John crystal. Drive straight through the town until you come to a sign saying that the road is closed ahead. **Turn left towards**

Edale

The village is almost a place of pilgrimage for long-distance walkers since the Pennine Way begins here, extending 250 miles northwards and ending in Scotland. However, two centuries ago few people visited the remote valley and only a handful of shepherds and farmers lived there, mainly in tiny settlements called 'booths'. If you look at the Outdoor Leisure or Landranger maps you will see that the name survives. Upper Booth is the westernmost settlement and then, as you descend Edale, there is Barber Booth, Grindsbrook Booth, Ollerbrook Booth and Nether Booth. All of them except Barber Booth are sited on the northern side of the valley in order to catch as much sunlight as possible. It seems likely that booths were originally the shelters used by herdsmen in the summer and that in time settlements grew up around them. The nearest church was at Castleton until a chapel-at-ease was built in 1633. Before this it must have been hard enough to attend Sunday worship, entailing a walk of 3 miles in each direction and a climb of 600 feet, but taking a corpse for burial would have called a dozen or so menfolk from the land to act as bearers over the coffin road to Castleton via Hollins

Cross. Until the eighteenth century Edale was a very self-contained community and most of the invariably large families relied on jaggers for contact with the world beyond their valley. Jaggers were packhorse merchants who bartered essentials such as salt and needles for woollen cloth. In 1795 new blood came to the vale with the setting up of a cotton mill on the River Noe. Workers were brought in from the cotton towns and accommodated in specially-built cottages near the mill but many women walked to work each day from Castleton. The mill was still working into the 1950s but has now been converted into holiday apartments. The building of the railway brought a final end to Edale's isolation and the impact on the community made by the several hundred navvies engaged to build the Cowburn tunnel must have been startling. Edale became one of the most popular destinations for Sunday walkers escaping by train from Sheffield or Manchester, and local entrepreneurs were soon busy catering for their needs. Many people of the between-the-wars generation will trace their love of walking to a first excursion into the hills from Edale, and fortunately this continues today as schoolchildren are brought from

different parts of the country to stay in Edale for study courses and to explore its countryside on foot.

Winnats Pass

The old theory that the pass is a collapsed cave system has been discredited and it is now thought that the landform was made when the waters of a vast lagoon were suddenly released, possibly by an earthquake. They pursued a tortuous course through the surrounding limestone forming the spectacular gorge. The road through the gorge was a turnpike route until a less steep road was built round Mam Tor in 1811. This had to be closed in 1977 after a landslip and today cars, but not lorries or coaches, use the pass as the only direct route between Castleton and the west. In 1758 the pass was the scene of a brutal murder when a young couple known only as Henry and Clara were murdered by five lead miners. They had eloped and were on their way to be married at Peak Forest when they met their deaths and their ghosts have haunted the pass ever since. One of the miners confessed to the murder as he was suffering a long and painful death, and it was then discovered that the lives of his four henchmen had also ended in a variety of horrible ways.

Speedwell and Blue John Caverns to climb up Winnats Pass. There is a stunning view of the pass as you approach it. Speedwell Cavern is to the left and there is a parking area opposite. **Go straight on at the top of the pass to join the B6061 going towards Sparrowpit.** You may well see hang gliders to the right as you approach this junction if the wind is in the right direction. The road passes the big quarry at Eldon Hill. Eldon Hole, one of the seven 'Wonders of the Peak' which were visited by eighteenth-century tourists, is a natural chasm 180 feet deep just to the south-east of the quarry. It can be reached on foot by a

footpath which goes from the north side of Eldon Hill to Peak Forest.

Pavilion Gardens, Buxton

At Sparrowpit F **keep straight on towards Manchester on A623,** passing Bennetstown Hall with its attractive pond. **At the A6 turn left to Buxton and pass through Dove Holes** where there are remains of circular earthworks resembling those of Arbor Low. Known as the Bull Ring, all of the standing stones have been used as building materials. The attractive approach to Buxton goes by the golf course with Fairfield church to the right. This is remarkable for having been built to the plans of the local schoolmaster in 1839. The road passes the Pavilion Gardens to reach Buxton town centre. ■

HATHERSAGE AND THE UPPER DERWENT VALLEY FROM BAKEWELL

START AND FINISH AT BAKEWELL
40 MILES – 2 HOURS

Bakewell claims to be the capital of the Peak District. It is not only the largest town but also has the headquarters of the National Park. The tour starts in the lovely old town and takes you to Hathersage where Little John is buried, then crosses moorland to the reservoirs of the upper Derwent (note that this valley can be very busy in summer). The return is via Bradwell and Monsal Head where the viaduct crossing the dale makes one long for the days of steam trains.

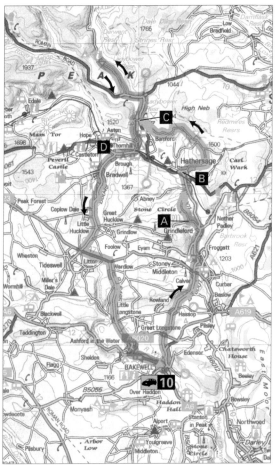

SCALE 1:250 000 OR 1 INCH TO 4 MILES *1 CM TO 2.5 KM*

Take the Chesterfield road out of Bakewell (A619) and cross the medieval bridge over the River Wye. About one mile out of town turn left on to the B6001 towards Hathersage. Go straight over the roundabout which follows after a further mile. There is lovely dales scenery as you come into Hassop with the long estate wall of Hassop Hall (now a hotel) to the left. The Catholic church in the middle of the village was built in severe classical style in 1816 for the Eyre family who lived at Hassop Hall. The road, fringed by masses of rhododendrons, gives very attractive views. The road dips down into Calver where the village is to the right. **Cross straight over the A623 at traffic lights, still heading to Hathersage.**

The road follows the west bank of the River Derwent to Grindleford. **Turn left on to the Hathersage road (B6001) soon after entering the village. Then, by the war memorial and opposite the Sir William pub, turn left again up Sir William Hill Road.** This road is not named after some notable local squire

but because it leads to Sir William Hill, 1,407 feet (422m). As you climb the road swings left and the trees end to the right. **Look carefully here to discover the unsignposted road to the** right **A** which goes through a beautiful wood and subsequently there are more lovely views through the trees into the Derwent valley. When it swings left and begins to descend there is a vista of Hathersage and the Hope valley. Hazelford Hall is the fine seventeenth- century farmhouse on the right and after this the lane gets more narrow as it descends, finally meeting the main road (B6001). **Bear left on to this.**

At Hathersage you meet the A625 at the junction. Turn right towards Sheffield. **Turn left at the end of the town** **B** **down School Lane (which has a weight restriction of 7½ tons) as the main road bends right.** You will pass the lane going up to the church on the left almost opposite the Scotsman's Pack inn. The road climbs steeply out of the village towards Higger Tor, but swings northwards near the top of the hill. **At a road**

• PLACES OF INTEREST •

Bakewell
In 1800 the Duke of Rutland transformed Bakewell, replacing many of its old timber-framed buildings with new ones of stone and building a large hotel (the Rutland Arms) at the centre of the town. He planned to make Bakewell a spa town to rival Buxton but his plans were always doomed to failure as the spring waters here, though rich in minerals, are cold and colourless. The Old House Museum, just above the church, occupies the sixteenth-century house built for the parson. The building has been carefully restored and visitors can see its wattle and daub walls and a variety of exhibits illustrating the ways of life in days gone by. The Market Hall dates from the early seventeenth century and was originally open to the street on one side. It is the information centre for the Peak National Park which has its headquarters in Bakewell in a large house on the Baslow Road. Bakewell grew up at the point where the River Wye could most easily be forded. Substantial earthworks were put up in the tenth century above the north-east bank of the river and the Normans built a more substantial stronghold within these defences. Nothing of this remains. The oldest of Bakewell's bridges is still in use and is crossed if you come to the town from the north or east. It dates from c.1300 and was widened in the nineteenth century. Holme Bridge, just upstream, is a packhorse bridge built in 1664 with low parapets to allow for the panniers carried by the horses.

Bakewell Old House Museum, off Church Lane. Open daily April–October, 2–5. Telephone: (01629) 813165.

Bakewell Puddings
Most important – never call them tarts in Bakewell. They were invented by accident. A cook at the Rutland Arms in the early nineteenth century was left to make a tart by the landlady who was expecting important guests. She mistakenly put the strawberry jam which was meant to be the topping at the bottom of the dish and poured an egg mixture over it. There must have been consternation when the dish was presented in the dining room but the guests were delighted and it soon proved to be a popular dish at the hotel. Later it became available from bakeries in the town and today there is a shop specialising in Bakewell Puddings from where they can be sent by post to anywhere in the world.

Little John of Hathersage
The innumerable place names to be found on the map around Hathersage which include the name of Robin Hood or his lieutenant, Little John, would seem to support the theory that Robin Hood came from Loxley, now a suburb of Sheffield. Unfortunately most of these names seem to have been coined in the eighteenth and nineteenth centuries, but the story of Little John's death at Hathersage has more substance. In 1625 a visitor to Hathersage church wrote of seeing his longbow hanging in the church. It was six feet long but was later taken to Canon Hall near Barnsley 'for safe keeping' and lost. Little John is supposed to have died in a tiny cottage just to the east of the church which was still standing in 1847. Its occupant then could remember Little John's grave in the churchyard being opened up in 1784 and a thighbone 30 inches long removed. This proved that a giant at least seven feet tall lay in the grave, though not one of ten feet or more which was his legendary height.

• PLACES OF INTEREST •

The Derwent Reservoirs
In 1901 work began on building the the two stone-faced dams of the Howden and Derwent reservoirs. They were constructed to supply water to Sheffield and the towns and cities of the East Midlands and work continued until 1916 with about a thousand workers living in 'Tin Town', a settlement of corrugated iron huts situated on the banks of the Derwent reservoir at Birchinlee. Conifers were planted around the reservoirs with some broad-leaved species. The larch, pine and spruce are now mature and are being harvested with native deciduous trees replacing them. However the two reservoirs were soon found to be inadequate and in 1935 dam builders moved in again to construct the Ladybower reservoir. This last phase of building lasted for ten years and necessitated flooding two villages – Ashopton and Derwent – as well as building viaducts to take the A57 and A6013 roads across arms of the reservoir. In May 1943, 617 Squadron of the RAF successfully bombed the Möhne and Eder dams in Germany. 53 members of the Dambuster squadron died in the raids and it is appropriate that a memorial to them is set up by the Derwent Dam, for the practice runs with Barnes Wallis' famous bouncing bomb were made here since the upper Derwent dams

bore remarkable similarity to the targets in Germany. In 1993, 80,000 people watched a lone Lancaster make a commemorative flight over the dams on the 50th anniversary of the raids. The upper Derwent valley is an area of exceptional man-made beauty and attracts 1.25 million visitors each year. They come to walk the shores of the reservoirs or the surrounding hills, to cycle, or just to enjoy the scenery. On fine summer weekends there are sometimes so many visitors that all the parking places get taken and drivers are turned away.

Monsal Head
From here you get one of the most memorable views in the Peak District with the high viaduct spanning the winding dale and the River Wye. It is hard to imagine the scene without the viaduct, which particularly incensed Ruskin when it was built. He would be even more annoyed to know that when the railway closed it was considered that the cost of demolishing it would be prohibitive and eventually part of the track was bought by the National Park and reinstated as the Monsal Trail, a footpath and cycleway. Since that time the viaduct has been made a listed structure. Ruskin wrote: 'The valley is gone and the Gods with it; and now, every fool in Buxton can

be at Bakewell in half-an-hour, and every fool in Bakewell at Buxton; which you think a lucrative process of exchange – you Fools Everywhere.'

Tip, the Faithful Collie
Joe Tagg was the Duke of Norfolk's shepherd for more than 40 years in the Derwent valley. He was famous for his dogs and the way he controlled them. Joe was a leading light at the early sheepdog trials, and in the 1920s received £1000 from an American buyer for one of his dogs. Joe had retired and was 86 when he went missing. He still lived in the upper Derwent valley and on 12 December 1953 was seen walking up the valley on the path to Slippery Stones with his collie Tip. When he failed to return a wide search was made of the lonely moors, but without success. Subsequent snowfall was heavy and his body was not discovered until the following March when a shepherd caught a glimpse of a dog he recognised as Tip on Ronksley Moor. The collie led him to the master she had guarded for 15 weeks, wearing a path as she circled his body. It was thought that the dog had survived by eating dead sheep and other carrion, and she was very thin and weak when found. Tip was 11 years old at the time and lived for further 2 years. A memorial stone to her stands close to the Derwent dam.

junction just after a cattle-grid turn left to Ladybower. Footpaths leave the road here to the right to climb Stanage Edge. **After ¹/₂ mile, just before a cattlegrid, turn right again following the sign towards Ladybower.** Hollin Bank car park is to the right just after this junction and an easy footpath leads up to Stanage Edge from here. Other footpaths descend to Hathersage through the beautiful North Lees estate. This was one of the properties owned by the Eyre family at Hathersage. Charlotte Brontë borrowed their name for *Jane Eyre* and turned Hathersage into the 'Morton' of the novel. She must have found the bleakness of the landscape here very similar to that around Haworth.

The road makes quite an abrupt turn to the left to cross a cattlegrid. **Shortly after this bear right off the main road to take a higher road to Ladybower which descends below the crags of Bamford Edge.** Suddenly a terrific view opens up over the Hope valley. There is a precipitous drop to the left as the road gradually descends to Bamford with Win Hill beyond, distinctive as being 'a hill on top of a hill'. **At the main road** **C** **turn right to the Ladybower Reservoir.**

There are banks of rhododendrons to the right with the Heatherdene car park sited above them as the road skirts the shore. The road crosses the viaduct over an arm of the reservoir to come to the A57. **Turn left towards Glossop. In about ¹/₂ mile, after crossing another viaduct, turn right to the Derwent Valley .**

The road follows the western shore of the reservoir and there are plenty of parking places (you are not permitted to stop elsewhere on the road or roadside). The Visitors' Centre is at Fairholmes below the Derwent Dam and at weekends and on Bank Holidays this is the end of the road. However, at other times

Howden Reservoir

you can drive on for another 5 miles to King's Tree at the top of the Howden Reservoir (when the road is closed to motorists you can take a minibus to the this point). Note that on summer weekends the valley is very busy and often all parking places are taken by 11 a.m.

Return by the Ladybower Reservoir, turn left on to the main road, and then take the first turning right to retrace your route across the viaduct and pass the Yorkshire Bridge Hotel and the lane descended earlier **C**. **A few yards past this junction turn right to Thornhill.** The road descends to cross the Yorkshire Bridge and then swings left. This is a very leafy part of the route as it closely follows the course of the river downstream. About a mile from the bridge there is a large car park on the left. **Soon after this the lane comes to the A625. Turn right.**

After almost one mile turn left **D** **on to the B6049 to Bradwell and Tideswell.** The road passes through the hamlet of Brough and then comes to Bradwell. On the far side of the village the road climbs up through Bradwell Dale, a lovely little

ravine. A turning to the left goes to Little Hucknall and the Gliding Club. After this the road runs through relatively flat countryside. **At the A623 turn left and then after about 1¹/₂ miles turn right on to the B6465 to Ashford and Wardlow.** This lonely spot, known fittingly as Wardlow Mires, was the site of a turnpike where the gatekeeper was murdered in 1815. A culprit was soon found for the crime – Anthony Lingard, aged 21, who was tried, found guilty, and duly executed at Derby. His corpse was hung in a gibbet cage at the scene of the crime until only the skeleton remained – he was the last felon to be gibbeted in this way in Derbyshire.

There are fine views to be seen from this road (B6465) which passes through Wardlow and soon after reaches the famous beauty spot of Monsal Head. The car park and tearoom are to be found on the right of the road. After this it is but a short drive to Ashford in the Water **where you turn left when you reach a main road by the Ashford Hotel. Turn right at the A6020 junction to cross the bridge, and then turn left on to the A6 to return to Bakewell.** ■

53

LONGDENDALE, STRINES AND THE SNAKE PASS FROM GLOSSOP

START AND FINISH AT GLOSSOP
46 MILES - 2 HOURS

The tour starts in the north-west of the county and begins by exploring Longdendale whose reservoirs supply Manchester and are an attractive part of the moorland landscape which predominates on this tour. The return to Glossop is via the Snake Pass where the scenery is often wooded and very reminiscent of the glens of Scotland.

From the town centre of Glossop take the B6105 northwards towards Barnsley and pass the station on the left. The road climbs out of the town – ignore a turn to Hadfield and Padfield on the left. At a point on the road known as the Devil's Elbow, Rhodeswood, the third of Longdendale's reservoirs, is seen to the left – there are five reservoirs altogether. The very

busy main road (A628) can be seen on the far side of the dale. The tortuous road slowly descends to Torside Reservoir, the largest of the group. Torside car park is to the right **A** opposite the sailing club near the end of the reservoir. The road runs below power lines before it swings left and then climbs a ramp to reach the main road close to the Woodhead Chapel,

dedicated to St James and founded in 1487. The roof of the little building has been robbed of its tiles and is at present covered in plastic sheeting. Sadly the building seems doomed to decay. Many of the 60 or so workers who died during the construction of the Woodhead Tunnel are buried in the graveyard. You can reach it by steps which lead up to the main road from the bottom of the ramp but be warned that crossing the road is hazardous.

Join the A628 B bearing right towards Barnsley. Woodhead Reservoir is to the right as a road goes off to the left to Holmfirth (A6024). Just over a mile after this junction there is a layby on the left as the Longdendale Trail crosses the road as it nears the top of the dale. To the right a track leads down to the portals of the two Woodhead railway tunnels. The coolest place on a hot day is close to the entrance to the tunnel when cool air blows through its three-mile length – high-voltage cables now run through the tunnels and not trains. To the left as you continue along the main road you see a wind farm and the distinctive TV mast on Holme Moss.

The summit of this high moorland road is reached at Fiddler's Green, about 1/2 mile after a road leaves to the left to Dunford Bridge. There used to be an inn at this desolate spot called the Plough and Harrow which flourished when the Woodhead Tunnel was being built but closed soon afterwards. One of its attractions was the music provided by a blind fiddler. One night he left the inn but became lost and was very fortunate to be found by a shepherd though his fiddle was lost. About a month later both fiddle and case were discovered and reunited with their owner. This strange event led to the pub changing its name and the area where it stood being marked as Fiddler's Green on current Ordnance Survey maps.

The entrance to Woodhead Tunnel

At the roundabout near the Flouch inn turn right **C** on to the A616 towards Sheffield. After ¹/₂ mile Langsett car park is to the left, and there is forest to the right with a second Langsett car park a little further on, nicely landscaped among the trees. **About 200 yards past this car park turn right D by the Wagon and Horses pub on the road signposted to Strines and Derwent Valley.** A lovely Gothic waterworks house is to the right before you cross Langsett dam while the valve house on the dam itself is supposed to be a replica of the gateway of Lancaster Castle. **Turn right when a road to Midhopestones goes off to the left, still heading for Strines.** As you pass Midhope reservoir there is forest to the left and open moorland to the right. **At a T-junction turn right E .**

A road leaves to the left to Bolsterstone and a very steep descent follows. Soon after this there is a view over Broomhead Reservoir. Keep straight on to pass another minor road leaving to the left which also goes to Bolsterstone via a hamlet with the name Wigtwizzle. Less than a mile further on yet another lane goes to the left by a milestone with the date 1730. **Stay on the main road past all these turnings.** There are beautiful views from

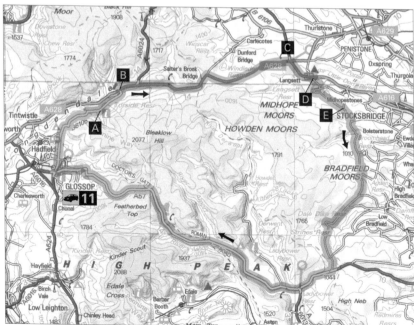

SCALE 1:250 000 OR 1 INCH TO 4 MILES *1 CM TO 2.5 KM*

The Roman road at Doctor's Gate

this road of Agden and Dale Dike reservoirs before the road runs through forest and then climbs to the Strines Inn. The remote pub must have been popular with drovers, carriers and packhorse teams in bygone days as it stands on an ancient north-to-south route through the Pennines. There was a house here in 1275 and in the sixteenth century the present building was the manor-house of the Worrall family whose coat of arms can be seen above the door. After the pub there is a stretch of desolate moorland, famous for its bilberries in late summer. A little way beyond the pub look to the left over Strines Reservoir to see Boot's Folly, the tower built in 1927 by Charles Boot to provide work for the

• PLACES OF INTEREST •

Glossop

Glossop seems like a town which has been shifted south-eastwards from the Lancashire cotton belt. Sensing this perhaps, the National Park sweeps in a wide arc around its boundaries to exclude it. The town is divided into distinct halves. Old Glossop is to the east of the town centre, and there are some charming old cottages here surrounding the church. This, though a medieval foundation, subsequently underwent three rebuildings – in 1853, 1914 and 1923. Glossop Hall was situated close to the church. Built by the Duke of Norfolk in 1850, it was demolished in 1960 and the grounds are now a public park. At the beginning of the century the eleventh Duke decided to build a new town to the west to accommodate workers employed in the cotton mills which were powered by the waters of the Glossop Brook. The new town was named Howard's Town after the Duke's family, and was planned around a fine town hall, built in 1838. By this time there were at least 46 mills strung along the streams. The town abandoned the Howard's Town name in 1876 to become Glossop. By then steam

power had replaced water power and a few large steam mills had taken the place of the numerous water-powered ones. Glossop went into decline as the cotton-spinning industry waned in the twentieth century. New industries have revived its fortunes in modern times. There are many advantages in living in Glossop, not least being its proximity to some of the best scenery of the Peak District. 3/4 mile to the north-west of the town centre is the Roman fort of Melandra Castle, known to the Romans as Ardotalia. This was an auxiliary fort built c. AD 75 and occupied until c.140. Only the foundations of the 19-acre site survive today.

Glossop Heritage Centre, Henry Street. Open weekdays and Saturdays, 10.30–4.30. Telephone: (01457) 869176.

Longdendale

The River Etherow flows westwards and eventually joins the River Mersey. The upper part of its course is through Longdendale where its waters were harnessed in five reservoirs – Bottoms, Valehouse, Rhodeswood, Torside and Woodhead. When they were completed in 1877 they formed

the largest man-made expanse of water in the world. Today the chain of reservoirs is North West Water's fifth largest resource and 30 million gallons a day flow from here to supply the needs of east Manchester. The dale was important as a packhorse route in medieval and Tudor times. In 1731 a turnpike road was constructed through the dale to link Cheshire with Yorkshire. Soon afterwards the waters of the River Etherow were used to power the waterwheels of cotton-spinning mills, and in 1839 work began on the railway between Manchester and Sheffield, the first trans-Pennine route. The line opened in 1845, the three-mile long Woodhead tunnel being one of the first wonders of the railway age. It was closed in 1981 even though a new tunnel had been opened in 1953, and the line electrified. Today the National Park and North West Water combine in looking after the valley on behalf of the public. In Longdendale there are facilities for walking, sailing, horse-riding and rock-climbing. Waymarked walking routes range from lakeside strolls to more energetic hillwalks giving panoramic views.

unemployed. The stately home above the reservoir which looks like a miniature Haddon Hall is Sugworth Hall. It is surrounded by masses of rhododendrons. The road crosses the boundary with Yorkshire and reaches the A57 at Moscar where the toll-house was the scene of a murder soon after the turnpike road was opened in 1821. The toll-keeper was killed but the murderer was soon caught and executed at Derby. After execution his body hung from a gibbet at this point where the old drovers' road from the north crossed the new turnpike.

At the A57, turn right towards Glossop. Pass the Ladybower Inn and keep ahead on the A57 to pass the A6013 which goes to Bamford. The main road crosses a viaduct over an arm of the reservoir. The site of Ashopton, a village which was flooded when the reservoir was constructed, is below you at this point. The road to the upper Derwent reservoirs leaves to the right at the end of the viaduct. The main road gives ever-changing views as it follows the shore of the Ladybower Reservoir to reach the beautiful Woodlands Valley. The Snake Pass Inn is almost at the top of this valley where the main road swings north to enter the Snake Plantations. The inn dates from 1749 and was originally called Lady Clough House but soon became known as the Snake Inn, because of the snake on the crest of the Duke of Devonshire, chairman of the turnpike trust which built the road.

After the Snake Pass Inn the A57 (part of a Roman road at this point) climbs through woods before swinging westwards to reach the summit of the pass just beyond Doctor's Gate where a stream has made a small ravine. There is a well-preserved section of the Roman road 1/2 mile to the north of the main road. Doctor's Gate gets its name from Doctor Talbot, the illegitimate son of the Earl of Shrewsbury who was vicar of Glossop between 1494 and

Glossop from the Snake Road

1550. He must often have come this way when he visited his father's castle at Sheffield where Mary, Queen of Scots was held prisoner and he was probably responsible for having sections of the Roman road repaired.

After the summit of the pass at 1,680 feet where the Pennine Way crosses the road, a sign warns of a long and steep descent. There is a grand view ahead over Glossop which was a town of many tall chimneys when its textile industry was at its height. Only four or five of these survive. Beyond is Greater Manchester. The road passes below a large quarry and so comes into the town where Old Glossop (and the parish church) is to the right before you reach the town centre. ■

• PLACES OF INTEREST •

The Snake Pass

As you speed across the Pennines on the A57 today, you may feel puzzled at the notoriety of the road and think that it owes its name to the series of sweeping bends it makes as it descends to Glossop. In fact the name comes from the emblem of the Duke of Devonshire who, with the Duke of Norfolk, was patron of the road. Its cost was enormous and it had only fifty years of use before the coming of the railways put paid to its profitability. Telford did the first survey for the route, but most work on it was undertaken by McAdam (father and son) with Josiah Fairbanks as surveyor in charge at its completion. The previous packhorse route from Sheffield was notoriously hazardous as it followed the Ashop Valley and then crossed the aptly-named Coldharbour Moor. In the early years of the nineteenth century the Duke of Norfolk was

planning to develop Glossop and badly needed to improve communications with industrial cities to the east and south. As the major landowner of the region the Duke of Devonshire shared his aims. When it was completed in 1821 it was the most scientifically constructed road of the age even though its surface, laid by gangs of Irish labourers, was no more than fist-sized chunks of limestone bound with limestone dust. However, this system proved its worth and lasted into the motor age, the surface only being covered with tar in 1930. Stakes driven into the ground provided a foundation over the worst of the peat bogs at the top of the pass. The Snake Road turnpike was already in decline in 1845 when in the month of September just one four-horse coach passed through the toll at Moscar, and the toll-keeper took only a little over £18 for the whole of the month.

LONGSHAW, EDALE AND STANTON IN PEAK FROM BASLOW

START AND FINISH AT BASLOW
60 MILES – 3 HOURS

The Hope Valley and Edale provide some of the best scenery in the Peak National Park. After this the route passes through Castleton and Tideswell before visiting lovely villages of the White Peak such as Monyash, Youlgreave and Stanton in Peak. To get the best from this tour stretch your legs to see beautiful Lathkill Dale or visit the Nine Ladies of Stanton Moor.

Leave Baslow on the A623 heading northwards towards Stockport and Manchester. Cliff College on the right was built in the nineteenth century as a seminary to train missionaries but is now used by lay people as well as those training for priesthood. **Two miles from Baslow turn right before Calver Bridge A to follow signs to Froggatt** and Curbar (if you miss the first turn take the next one on the other side of the new bridge). **Take the road directly opposite the Bridge Inn and immediately fork left following a signpost to Froggatt and Sheffield and passing a long wooden building.** This is the Duke's Drive which runs above a section of the river known as The Goyt, built to divert water to power Arkwright's Calver Mill, well seen across the river from the road. **The Drive follows the river for a short way before bearing left into Riddings Lane and then climbing a hill to reach the B6054. Turn right towards Hathersage and Sheffield.** The crags of Froggatt Edge are seen to the right as you drive through Froggatt village. The road goes through lovely woods and climbs steadily. An old hunting lodge is to be seen on the skyline ahead, which might have been the destination for the Duke on his drive except that it is part of the Longshaw estate which belonged to the Duke of Rutland rather than the Duke of Devonshire. There is a car park to the left by the junction where the Chesterfield road (B6054) goes off to the right. **Bear left here towards Sheffield.** There is another National Trust car park just after the junction at a place with the intriguing name of Wooden Pole. The original wooden pole here served as a guide post on the Dronfield to Tideswell packhorse route. **Head for Hathersage and Castleton on the B6055 when the B6450**

• *PLACES OF INTEREST* •

Baslow
Like many another Derbyshire town and village Baslow set up its own hydro in the 1880s. For more than forty years people came to Baslow to take its cure, but although two large hotels which once served the spa are still in operation, no trace of the hydro survives. St Anne's church is picturesque in its riverside setting but has been much restored. The nearby seventeenth-century bridge has a tiny tollhouse with a door only 40 inches high.

Longshaw Estate
There are 1,600 acres of National Trust land here centred on Longshaw Lodge, a shooting lodge built in 1827 for the Duke of Rutland (not open). Sheepdog trials held in a meadow below the lodge each September are the oldest in the country, having started in 1898. The estate provides walkers with a grand variety of scenery, from the ancient woodland of Padley Gorge to the moorland of White Edge which at 1,267 feet is its highest land. Millstone grit is the predominant rock and more than 200 millstones line the track above Bolehill quarries, abandoned when the trade in them died in the 1920s. The Visitors' Centre, shop and cafeteria are open throughout the year (but only at weekends in winter). Telephone: (01433) 631708 (Visitors' Centre) or (01433) 631757/670368 (Warden's office).

branches to the right to Sheffield. **The main car park for the Longshaw Estate is on the left B just before you meet the A625.**

Turn left on to the A625 towards Castleton. The famous Toad's Mouth Rock is close to road on the right just after it crosses the Burbage Brook. A new car park and picnic area have been made to the right just before the road swings right and Surprise View is revealed from the top of Millstone Edge. Footpaths climb to the right and you can follow these to get close-up views of the grotesquely-weathered tors. The official Surprise Viewpoint is to the south of the road above the sheer rock faces of the disused Bolehill quarries. There is a fine view of Hathersage church as you approach the village. It is beautifully sited on a small hill to overlook Hathersage from the north. Little John's grave in the churchyard attracts many visitors (see page 51).

Keep on the A625 to drive westwards through the village and pass Bamford, where the road to Ladybower (A6013) goes off to the right. 2¹/₂ miles further on at Hope turn right opposite the fourteenth-century church C to Edale.

Lose Hill is the fine pointed hill to the left as the road twists round to follow the course of the little River Noe upstream. The ridge to the left descends steeply from Lose Hill to reach the saddle at

Hollins Cross which was where the coffin road from Edale to Castleton crossed. Most people prefer the scenery going westwards up Edale. In Victorian times there were proposals to make a reservoir out of the valley. It may have been geological considerations which defeated the plan or the fact that the railway already ran through Edale.

There is a café at Edale station and more refreshment is available in the village itself. The car park is to the right close to the lane into the village, and it is best to leave your car here as there are no other car parks. In the village the Old Nag's Head pub is the official start of the Pennine Way.

Carry on along the road to pass a turn to the right to Upper Booth, the topmost of Edale's original settlements, all called 'booths'. After this the road begins to climb

quite steeply and if conditions are favourable you will see hang gliders and parascenders flying from Mam Tor – the Shivering Mountain. It is called this because its layers of shale sandwiched between bands of gritstone make it prone to landslips, one of which permanently closed the main road which used to run round the hill to connect Castleton with Chapel-en-le-Frith and provided an easier gradient than Winnats Pass. **From the crest just below Mam Tor the road descends to the A625. Turn left to Castleton.**

Mam Nick car park and picnic site is immediately to the left and the turn to the Blue John Cavern on the left ¹/₂ mile further on. This is the old main road blocked by a landslide many years ago. **About ¹/₄ mile after this turn left D following the sign to Castleton down Winnats Pass.**

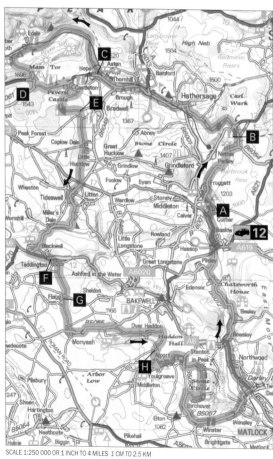

SCALE 1:250 000 OR 1 INCH TO 4 MILES *1 CM TO 2.5 KM*

Winnats Pass

The steepness is more apparent going down with fingers of jagged rock jutting within touching distance of the road. Speedwell Cavern is to the right as the descent eases and there is a car park opposite. **At a main road turn right to Castleton** – the Treak Cliff Caverns are to the left at this junction. As you enter Castleton the Peak Cavern is to the right.

The main car park is on the left. **Just after this take the road on the right opposite the Bull's Head to go by the Castle Inn and the church. Bear left to pass the pretty little square and follow the road up the hill. Do not take the lane which forks to the left but keep on climbing steeply through trees.** When these end there is a beautiful view over the valley. Ignore another lane to the left and after the road swings sharply to the right there is a convenient layby where you can pause to look back to Castleton and the Hope Valley.

The road crosses Dirtlow Rake, a stretch of very desolate moorland. Keep on the main road following the sign to Little Hucklow. The road does a wide sweep with the chimney of the cement works always to the left. **At a T-junction just after a quarry turn right E to Little Hucklow.** A road to Bradwell goes off to the left – at this point there is a lovely panorama with a random pattern of stone walls covering the daleside. Little Hucklow is reached by a steep lane to the left **but keep on the major road for another 2 miles to meet the A623 by the Anchor inn. Cross the main road to follow the sign to Tideswell. Drive straight through the delightful town** unless you wish to pause for

• PLACES OF INTEREST •

Caves at Castleton
Peak Cavern, whose grand 50-foot high entrance is below the hill on which Peveril Castle stands, has been known to tourists for hundreds of years. Cottages were built in the cave mouth and soot from their chimneys can still be seen on the roof. There was also a ropewalk, probably established here because workers could make the ropes under cover, and relics of this are also on show. Visitors to the cave walk for a mile underground seeing en route the 100-foot-high Great Cave and descending to the River Styx which was once, as its name suggests, thought to be the entrance to Hades. Open Easter–October 10–5 (but closed on Mondays in low season). Telephone: (01433) 620285.

Treak Cliff Cavern is famous for its displays of stalactites and stalagmites in the well-named Dream and Aladdin Caves and for its veins of Blue John. The climax of a tour here is the chamber known as 'The Dome of St Paul's' where the ceiling is 40 feet high and ablaze with colour. Open daily except Christmas Day, March–October 9.30–5.30, November–February 9.30–4. Telephone: (01433) 620571.

Speedwell Cavern
Visitors are taken 1/2 mile through the system by motor boat. They disembark at the Bottomless Pit Cavern, a vast cave with a high ceiling and an unfathomable hole. Open daily except Christmas Day, 9.30–5.30 in summer, and 9.30–4.30 in winter. Telephone: (01433) 620512.

Blue John Cavern
This has a succession of spectacular chambers with veins of Blue John prominent. The Waterfall Cavern is a cascade of limestone which looks just like a frozen waterfall while Lord Mulgrave's Dining Room got its name from a banquet set up there

in the last century by the peer with the help of local lead miners. The entrance is at the top of Winnat's Pass. Open daily except Christmas, 9.30–5.30 or dusk (and in January and February only open if road conditions are favourable). Telephone: (01433) 620642.

The Nine Ladies
Stanton Moor is a high and isolated area of gritstone surrounded by limestone. More than 70 prehistoric burial sites litter the moor, the most prominent being the Nine Ladies, a circle of stones (much smaller than those of Arbor Low) which is just 35 yards in circumference. A much larger monolith stands about 50 yards away and is known as the King Stone which gives rise to the legend (and there are many other similar stories throughout Britain) that the King was a fiddler who played for the Nine Ladies on the Sabbath, the consequence being that all were turned to stone.

refreshment or investigate its numerous craft shops.

The road descends Tideswell Dale. There is a car park and picnic site on the left about a mile out of the town. In another mile you reach Miller's Dale where the car park is on the road to the right after the viaduct. **Continue on the B6049 and turn left at the A6 to Matlock and Bakewell. Pass the Waterloo pub and then turn right ◼ to Taddington at the second of two turns offered close together on a short section of dual carriageway.**

Taddington is a charming upland village, and you may like to explore it **even though the route lies away from it, turning up Humphrey Gate on the right as you enter the village to head for Flagg and Monyash.** The road goes above Taddington and later gives wide views as it follows the crest of the hill. After 1½ miles you come to a crossroads. **Go straight over to Flagg and Monyash but about 200 yards after this turn left ◼ to Monyash (the road ahead goes to Flagg).** This is a lovely road through a shallow dale which was an active lead mining area in the past. The steeple of Monyash church can be seen ahead before **you reach the B5055 where you turn left towards Bakewell and go through Monyash** which has tearooms and a pub.

After 2 miles turn right off the B5055 to Over Haddon

and Lathkill Dale when the main road swings left after a farm. There is a car park to the right as you come into Over Haddon where you can leave your car and take the short walk down to Lathkill Dale, one of the prettiest of all the dales. **In Over Haddon turn left at a T-junction by the Lathkill Dale Craft Centre and then take the first turn right signposted to Youlgreave. At a T-junction opposite a farm turn right, still following the sign to Youlgreave.** This is an enjoyable part of the route which descends round a hairpin bend to the beautiful Conksbury Bridge over the River Lathkill. This is always a popular place for ramblers to pause and there is cow parsley everywhere in the summer – even the meadows are full of it.

As the road climbs from the bridge look for a lane on the left ◼, signposted to Youlgreave. Take this turn – the lane comes out in the middle of the village by the church. Turn left to pass the school and descend a steep hill into beautiful Alport. Turn right towards Ashbourne on the B5056 and then after ½ mile turn left to Stanton in Peak. Stanton is a delightful village and many visitors will be puzzled by the name of its pub, the Flying Childers. This is the name of a famous racehorse owned by the fourth Duke of Devonshire. **Keep on the main road through the**

village heading for Birchover. There are soon fine views to the right and to the left there is space to park, should you like to see the prehistoric sites on Stanton Moor, the most famous being the Nine Ladies stone circle.

Go through Birchover keeping on the main road through the village to meet the B5056 and turn left towards Ashbourne. The limestone crags to the right are Robin Hood's Stride and a Hermit's Cave is also to be found here. **After about 1½ miles of twisty road bear left to take the B5057 and come to Winster. Pass Winster church and the old market hall (National Trust) and continue through the village on to Wensley, passing through Wensley Dale which is not to be confused with the one in Yorkshire. Cross the Derwent over Darley Bridge into Darley Dale.** The Red House Stables Working Carriage Museum is to the right and Darley Dale station (Peak Rail) to the left. **Turn left on to the A6 towards Rowsley.**

Turn right at Rowsley on to the B6012 to Baslow and Chatsworth. Beeley village is to the right with the lovely church a little further on. **Go over the narrow bridge into Chatsworth park.** A car park is on the left. The spire of Edensor church ahead is almost as much of an eye-catcher as Chatsworth House to the right. If you time your visit right you will see the fountain throwing its jet of water 200 feet into the air – high above the trees. Edensor owes its appearance to the sixth Duke not knowing which style of architecture he best liked, so Paxton designed every house differently. **Keep on the main road when the Bakewell road goes off to the left and so come back to Baslow, turning left at the roundabout on the A623 to reach the centre of the village.** ◼

Nine Ladies Stone Circle, Stanton Moor

WETTON AND THE MANIFOLD VALLEY FROM ALSOP EN LE DALE

START AND FINISH AT ALSOP EN LE DALE
36 MILES – 2 HOURS

This short tour takes you into Staffordshire where the valley of the River Manifold proves to be almost as beautiful as Dove Dale but without quite so many people. Longnor is an old market town which remains sleepy and unspoilt in its isolation, and the return leg of the route is through some of the loveliest scenery of the White Peak.

The tour starts from the Alsop en le Dale Station picnic area car park, on the east side of the A515 about 6 miles north of Ashbourne. **From the car park cross the A515 on to the lane opposite following the sign to Milldale and Alstonefield. At the bottom of the steep hill turn right and descend into Wolfscote Dale to cross the county boundary on the bridge over the River Dove. Keep on the main road** towards Alstonefield, forking to the right.

At Alstonefield the church, with its small tower, battlements and pinnacles, can be seen to the left as you near the village. The pub (The George) is also to the left

Wolfscote Dale

overlooking the green. **Turn left after the pub car park following the sign to Wetton and Ilam. Keep straight on at a major road in the middle of the village to come to a second major road by Yew Tree Farm and turn left here, again towards Wetton and Ilam. The lane drops down into Hope where, at the bottom of the hill just before the pub, you take the road to the right A to Wetton. Keep to the main road to reach this village.** The church has a sturdy medieval tower but was otherwise rebuilt in Georgian times.

From Wetton head for Wettonmill (Wetton Mill on signposts) and Butterton, keeping on the main road to pass the church and the pub on the left and ignoring turnings to Grindon. The valley appears ahead with the steeple of Grindon church beyond. Thor's Cave can also be seen, one of the most spectacular features of the dales. A footpath goes to the cave from Wetton but be warned that the rock on its threshold is well worn and very slippery when wet. The cave is 60 feet wide and was occupied by man in the Iron Age and during the Roman occupation when the lead mines around Wetton were being worked.

The lane down to Wettonmill is steep, narrow and twisting as well as being busy with cars, cyclists and walkers, especially on summer weekends. There is a car park at the bottom of the hill. It is optional whether you choose to cross the bridge here or not – if you do you will find the lane following the River Manifold on its western bank more narrow than the one on the other side and you will have to splash through a ford when the roads rejoin in about ¼ mile or so.

Head for Warslow after the roads join again on the lane following the river. There are lots of places here where you can park near the riverbank. It is a popular venue with children, who

also find excitement with the tunnel which you come to in about a mile. This is about 200 yards long and has refuges for pedestrians or cyclists. However, it is well lit and should not present any difficulties as long as motorists are patient and wait for a clear way through.

After the tunnel bear right B and then turn left to cross the bridge to head for Hulme End. The road continues to follow the Manifold Valley towards Ecton. A road to Warslow leaves to the left and one to the right leads off to Back of Ecton. **At a main road turn left to Hulme End and Hartington and you will come to the B5054 by the Manifold Valley Hotel. Turn right on to the main road for 300 yards before turning left to Sheen and Longnor.** Sheen Hill, topped by a rocky tor, overlooks the village. Sheen church was rebuilt in 1850,

partially by William Butterfield who is famous for his heavy Gothic work on Cambridge colleges and Anglo-Catholic churches in London. He also built a large parsonage at Sheen which is an excellent example of his architectural style.

Thor's Cave

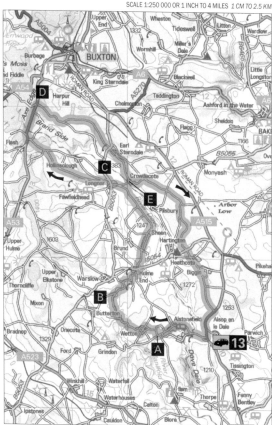

Alstonefield

The parish is large today, but was once even bigger, taking in all of the land between the Rivers Dove and Manifold. Until the building of the turnpikes it was a place of some importance, standing at the junction of several busy packhorse routes. Alstonefield was granted a market charter in 1308 and cattle sales continued in the village until the early years of this century. Modern means of transport left the village stranded on its 900-foot-high hillside but few of the villagers living at Alstonefield today would think that a bad thing. There are many fine cottages with mullion windows, a popular pub and a church founded in the ninth century where examples of Saxon carving are still to be found. Most of the fabric is of Norman or medieval date, and there is much flamboyant seventeenth-century woodwork to be seen in the two-decker pulpit and the box pews. The Cotton Pew is a reminder that Charles Cotton, who worked with Izaak Walton on *The Compleat Angler*, was a local squire and worshipped here.

Longnor

Like Alstonefield, Longnor suffered from being cut off from modern means of transport – main road, canal and railway. Similarly this gives it an unspoilt charm. However, when compared with Alstonefield it is clearly a town, albeit a tiny one, and not a village. The Market Hall which fronts the cobbled square dates from 1873 and was built at the height of the town's prosperity when Longnor had more than 550 inhabitants. A hundred years later there were about 360 and most of the inns which had previously served the market-goers had closed. However Longnor is a conservation area within the National Park and its location amidst oustanding scenery and its charm attract many summer visitors. The Market Hall now serves as a craft centre.

After Sheen there is a lovely view to the right into the Dove valley. The tiny village of Pilsbury can be seen with the earth ramparts of its motte-and-bailey castle on the hilltop to the north. The road now follows the ridge between the Manifold and Dove valleys and the view opens up as it dips down towards Longnor. **Bear left at a major road as you come to the village and at the main road in the centre of the village (B5053) turn right towards Buxton. Climb the hill past the school and the fire station and, just before the de-restriction sign, turn left  C to Hollinsclough and Flash. Keep on the main road when a lane to Hollinsclough goes off to the right.** This is a good ridge road across Hollinsclough Moor. The A53 can be seen on the skyline ahead. There is a viewpoint layby to the left as the road begins to descend to the main road at Flash Bar. This is where the turnpike was situated, the village being reached by a lane off the main road just to the south. Flash claims to be England's highest village, standing at 1,518 feet, and in bygone days was a refuge for fugitives and counterfeiters – hence the term 'flash money'. Being situated very close to the boundaries of three counties it was easy for them to evade capture by moving into an adjacent county when the law officers of another county approached.

Turn right on to the A53 and re-enter Derbyshire. The River Dove rises to the right of the road very close to the boundary. **Pass a turn to Brand Side on the right and take the next turn right D at staggered crossroads following the sign to Dalehead. Cross a cattle-grid after about 2 miles and bear left when the road forks to Earl Sterndale.** The road passes a large quarry on the left before coming to Harley Grange Farm. A little further on you see Parkhouse Hill, the fine summit to the right, and High Wheeldon ahead, directly behind Earl Sterndale church.

Cross the B5053 into Earl Sterndale passing the Quiet Woman pub and the church. Follow the main road downhill – High Wheeldon is the pointed hill on the left. It belongs to the National Trust and is a fine viewpoint. Fox Hole Cave is on its north-west flank and was inhabited by man for thousands of years from Palaeolithic until Roman times. **At the T-junction at Crowdecote E turn left to climb the hill. There is a**

Longnor

The pub sign at Earl Sterndale

beautiful view to the right. **Turn right at the crossroads at High Needham to Pilsbury and Hartington.**

Go straight on at the next crossroads heading towards Hartington. The delightfully-named Custard Field Farm has an enormous silo, making it easy to distinguish. **Keep straight on when a road goes left to Parsleyhay and Newhaven and in ¹/₂ mile branch left to stay on the main road, still heading for Hartington, when a lesser road goes ahead.** You are now driving through Long Dale. **After 1³/₄ miles you come to the B5054. Cross this to follow the sign to Heathcote and Biggin. A lane goes to Heathcote to the left – keep to the major road here, and nearly a mile further on when another road leaves to Biggin. Just after the railway bridge which takes the Tissington Trail over the route, turn right on to the A515 to return to the car park at Alsop en le Dale.** ■

• PLACES OF INTEREST •

Earl Sterndale
This tiny, remote village would seem to make an unlikely target for an air-raid yet on 9 January 1941 St Michael's church was destroyed by incendiary bombs (in fact the target was an ammunition dump hidden in a nearby quarry). However, eleven years later the church was restored and even the Saxon font, shattered by the bombs, had been repaired. On the Sunday nearest to 11 October the annual Wakes are held in the village to celebrate a church festival. On the previous Friday the man found to be most drunk is elected mayor of the village for a year. This may sound sexist but so is the pub sign, the Quiet Woman, where a headless woman is shown below the inscription 'Soft words turneth away wrath.' High Wheeldon, the beautiful hill just to the south-east of the village and, at

1100 feet, a wonderful viewpoint, was given to the National Trust as a war memorial to the men of Derbyshire and Staffordshire regiments who gave their lives in two world wars.

The Manifold Valley
Just as Derbyshire shares part of the Peak District with Yorkshire, the county shares some of the best of its dales scenery with Staffordshire. While the River Dove forms the county boundary for much of its course, all of the valley of the River Manifold falls within Staffordshire. The Manifold rises close to the source of the Dove on Axe Edge and flows through a broad valley until it reaches limestone at Hulme End. From here its course is spectacular as it winds through a succession of well-wooded gorges, their sides riddled with caves. The best

known of these is Thor's Cave situated on the side of the gorge 250 feet above the river, but there are also Ossom's Cave, where flints were worked in prehistoric times, and Elderbush Cave which was inhabited by man in the Stone Age. The Manifold, like its tributary the little River Hamps, has one disconcerting habit – in summers when the weather has been dry it disappears down swallets to flow underground, leaving its stream-bed dry. The Manifold Way is the footpath and cycle route which follows the valleys of the rivers Manifold and Hamps along the former track of the Leek and Manifold Light Railway. This narrow-gauge line was only in existence for thirty years from 1904, its locos being based on an Indian design. It was built to serve a big dairy at Ecton, collecting milk from farms in the valley.

GAWSWORTH HALL, BIDDULPH GARDENS AND THE ROACHES FROM BUXTON

START AND FINISH AT BUXTON
60 MILES – 3 HOURS

This three-counties tour also goes through three towns, each full of character as well as fine buildings. Cheshire is famous for its black-and-white buildings and Gawsworth Hall is an outstanding example amongst these. No garden-lover will want to leave the district without seeing those at Biddulph Grange – their restoration is a triumph for the National Trust. Add to this the grand scenery of The Roaches and you have the best ingredients for a memorable drive.

From the centre of Buxton, with The Crescent to the left, head towards Leek, Congleton and Macclesfield on the A53. At a roundabout by the Devonshire Royal Hospital the road to Whaley Bridge (A5004) leaves to the right. **Keep ahead here, still** on the A53, to pass the church of St John the Baptist to the right and the Opera House on the left. About 1½ miles from the town centre the A53 road to Leek carries on ahead. **Turn right off the main road on the A54 to Congleton and** Macclesfield. After a further 1½ miles the A537 to Macclesfield leaves to the right. Remain on the A54 here too, which enters Cheshire amid wild moorland scenery. As you come to a group of fir trees (after 5½ miles) look

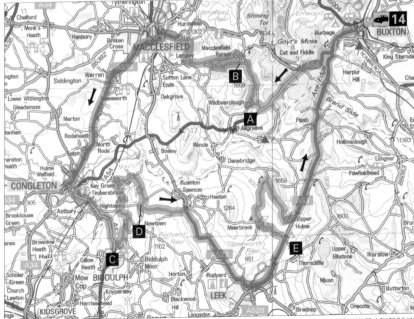

SCALE 1:250 000 OR 1 INCH TO 4 MILES *1 CM TO 2.5 KM*

The Forest Chapel decorated with rushes

for a turn to the right **A** to Wildboarclough. Take this road which runs through banks of rhododendrons and bear left when the road forks. There is a tall estate wall to the right. The road drops down into Wildboarclough passing the church. **Turn right at a T-junction having crossed the bridge over the Clough Brook** (the pub is to the left here).

The road follows the stream through the dale and there are vistas of gently rounded hills. There is a parking place just before a modern bridge where a

• PLACES OF INTEREST •

The Church of St Stephen, Macclesfield Forest

More commonly known as Forest Chapel, the first chapel at this remote spot was built in 1673 to serve the widespread local community which otherwise had to travel to Macclesfield to worship or bury the dead. The present building dates from 1834 and is chiefly famous for its rush-bearing ceremony which takes place on the first Sunday after 12 August and attracts large crowds. Rushes were originally spread on the floors of churches to keep them dry and warm, though the practice seems to have been dropped after the Great Plague of 1665–66 in many districts. At this chapel it has been going on for as long as anyone can remember, and the rushes are plaited and intertwined with flowers to decorate the church as well as being spread on the floor. They are left for a week before being cleared away.

Tegg's Nose Country Park

A tegg is the local name for a yearling sheep and the shape of the hill resembles that of a sheep's head so the derivation is obvious. The quarry here provided a reddish gritstone often used as setts in the streets of industrial towns but it was closed in 1955 when it was seen that the summit of the hill was being taken away. The exposed rock face is now a climbing and abseiling ground and

the park provides a variety of trails of varying length as well as a picnic area and café. Rangers' Office telephone: (01625) 614279.

Macclesfield

In Norman and medieval times the town lay on the edge of a large game reserve used by royalty and nobility (Macclesfield Forest) and though granted a market charter in 1261 it does not seem to have flourished greatly until the establishment of the first silk mill beside the River Bollin in 1743. The first factory simply wrapped buttons in silk, but a little later the influx of Huguenot weavers from France brought new techniques to Macclesfield and the textile industry grew. Macclesfield has an excellent market which is held on Tuesdays, Fridays and Saturdays. The Silk Museum is the only one of its kind in the country and illustrates all aspects of silk production. You can also visit Paradise Mill which has 26 hand looms operated by guide-demonstrators.

Macclesfield Silk Museum, Heritage Centre, Roe Street. Open Monday–Saturday 11–5. Summer Sundays 1–5 (but 1–4 November–February). Telephone: (01625) 613210.

Paradise Mill, Park Lane. Open Tuesday–Sundays and Bank Holidays 1–5 (but 1–4 November–February). Telephone: (01625) 618228.

Gawsworth Hall

The beautiful building dates from 1480 as the home of the Fitton family. Mary Fitton, briefly lady-in-waiting to Queen Elizabeth I, may have been Shakespeare's 'Dark Lady' of the sonnets. She was imprisoned in the Tower of London by the Queen after being made pregnant by the Earl of Pembroke but was later able to return to Gawsworth. In the late seventeenth century the house was reduced in size by the second Earl of Macclesfield. A duel was fought at Gawsworth in 1712 between Lord Mohun and the Duke of Hamilton over the estate, which, after both were killed in the duel, was subsequently owned by the Stanhopes, earls of Harrington. The black and white building is finely furnished and has family portraits from all periods. Its beautiful chapel has stained glass by Burne-Jones. One of England's great eccentrics was Samuel 'Maggoty' Johnson, the last professional jester who lived at Gawsworth, died there in 1773, and is buried in Maggoty Wood near the house. The inscription on his grave says that he preferred to be buried here on his own – otherwise on Judgement Day he might quarrel with the occupant of a neighbouring grave over the ownership of a bone!

Open daily second week in April–first in October, 2–5.30. Telephone: (01260) 223456.

Gawsworth Hall

road joins from the right. A little
further on there is another
parking place in Vicarage Quarry.
**After 1/2 mile take the turning
left off the main road to
Langley to reach a crossroads
[B] where there is a stone
plaque to Walter Smith, the
local historian who died in
1948.** There is a car park a few
yards down the lane to the right.
**Here there is a choice of
routes. Turn right and then
bear left at the next junction
to visit the famous
Macclesfield Forest Chapel, or
go straight ahead to the picnic
place (and toilets) at
Trentabank Reservoir.** This is
one of the four reservoirs which

tap the waters of the River Bollin
before it reaches Macclesfield. Of
course it is also easy to visit
chapel and reservoir. Both roads
lead to Langley and meet by
Leathers Smithy pub at the end of
Ridgegate Reservoir.

**Go through Langley's
narrow main street and,
having passed a chapel on the
left, look for a well-concealed
and unsignposted turn to the
right at the village hall.** This
lane crosses the little River Bollin
and then climbs steeply. Take care
in negotiating the series of sharp
bends. There is a fine view from
the top of the hill. At a T-junction
another choice is presented.
Either turn left and follow the

road to join the A537 to
Macclesfield, or turn right for
3/4 mile to visit Tegg's Nose
Country Park.** From here
footpaths lead up to the top of the
gritstone hill which is an
outstanding viewpoint.

**From Macclesfield head for
Congleton on the A536. About
3 miles out of town, and
shortly after entering a
50mph limit, turn left at a
crossroads down Church Lane
to Gawsworth Hall.** As you
approach the hall note Maggoty
Lane on the right, named after
Gawsworth's famous jester.

**From the hall return to the
A536 by turning left at
crossroads down Maggoty
Lane past Maggoty Wood and
then turn left to drive 41/2
miles to Congleton. Follow
the signs to the town centre
and then head to Biddulph on
the A527.** Congleton is a busy
and prosperous market town
largely retaining its medieval
street-plan as well as a few black-
and-white buildings. The town
suffered badly from plague in
1601 and 1641, losing three
quarters of its population.

**The A527 crosses a railway
and nearly 3 miles further on
reaches the entrance to
Biddulph Grange gardens.
This is in Grange Road which
is to the left [C] after the main
road makes a sweeping Z-
bend as it comes to the 30
mph limit. Once in Grange
Road the entrance to the
garden is immediately on the
right.**

**Carry on along this road
past the entrance to the
Country Park on the right and
the Talbot pub on the left
following the signposts to
Biddulph Park and Leek.** The
road climbs steadily to pass an
ancient roadside cross and a
radio mast, both on the left.
Ignore a turning to the right to
Leek, keeping ahead towards
Timbersbrook. There is a fine
view to the left with the radio
telescope at Jodrell Bank usually

The Chinese Garden at Biddulph Grange

clearly visible. **Go straight over a crossroads, still heading for Timbersbrook.** The Cloud is the wooded hill to the right which is seen as you begin to drop down into Timbersbrook. **At the next junction, by a telephone box, turn right to Bosley.** The pleasant lane climbs round The Cloud following the curve of the hill. There are magnificent views to the left. **Keep on the main road when Pedley Lane goes off to the left and about 1/4 mile after this turn right at a crossroads.** The road continues to climb and swing round The Cloud until it reaches the eastern flank and its topmost crags can be seen. At the top of the road there is a small car park and a footpath leaves to the summit. **Keep on the main road when a byway goes off to the left to Woodhouse Green and continue for another 300 yards to a main road** **where you turn left to Rushton and Leek. The road descends steadily – go straight over crossroads by the Crown Inn to come to the A523 at Ryecroft Gate. Turn right to pass Rudyard Reservoir** (where an attraction is the steamer which gives trips from the Damhead) **and continue on the A523 to Leek.**

The road passes through the town centre. **Take the A53 (Buxton) road out of Leek.** The Roaches can soon be seen ahead – startling silhouettes on the skyline. A roadside notice says: 'Limited parking at the Roaches, park and drive at weekends'. **2 1/2 miles from Leek, at the Three Horseshoes Inn, turn left to Meerbrook** [E]. As you come to Meerbrook the entrance to Tittesworth Reservoir is to the left. This provides the Pottery towns and dates from 1858 but was reconstructed 1959–63 when the water level was raised. It takes water from the River Churnet and provides an excellent habitat for waders and meadow birds. There

• *PLACES OF INTEREST* •

Leek

Many people find the little town to be rather like a Lancashire cotton town, with its steep cobbled streets and old mills. However there are few towns in the northern county which have such a wealth of Georgian houses. There is also a fine market place and an interesting medieval church. Like Macclesfield, Leek's first mills produced silk but these were soon joined by cotton mills and by the corn mill built by James Brindley in 1752. Much of his original machinery has been re-installed and the watermill is now able to work again. The building also houses a museum devoted to Brindley.

Brindley Mill, Mill Street. Open Easter–October, weekends and Bank Holiday Mondays, 2–5. Telephone: (01538) 384195/383211.

Biddulph Grange Gardens

At Biddulph Grange the National Trust has made a stunning reconstruction of the high Victorian garden, acquired in 1988. It covers 15 acres and includes a colourful Chinese bridge and pavilion, as well as a wide-ranging collection of plants. Paths embanked with the twisted roots of felled trees lead through tunnels into gardens of contrasting character from those seen before. Guided tours and restaurant. Open April–October,

Wednesdays–Fridays noon–6. Saturdays, Sundays and Bank Holidays 11–6. Also open at weekends in November and December. Telephone: (01782) 517999.

The Roaches

The scalloped ridge, an outcrop of millstone grit, rises to a height of 1,657 feet at its northern end. It is a wonderful viewpoint for walkers and gives rock climbers a wide choice of pitches. Since 1975 the National Trust has

owned 975 acres of the ridge and if you are very quiet and observant you may be fortunate in seeing a wallaby here. A small colony of these creatures has survived here since the outbreak of the Second World War when the owner of a private zoo was called up and the wallabies eventually escaped from their enclosure.

are also areas of woodland to add more interest to the nature trail.

Continue into Meerbrook and turn right immediately after the Lazy Trout Inn. The lane heads towards the Roaches, bending sharply right after nearly a mile when a private road goes ahead. It snakes up towards the crages, finally reaching a T-junction. **Turn right to pass below the Roaches.** There is only limited parking here – rock climbers arrive early and take many of the spaces. There are magnificent views south and west over Tittesworth and Rudyard

reservoirs. After the Roaches Tearoom the road descends steadily to pass the old yarn-dyeing mill at Upper Hulme and comes to a T-junction at the top of a small rise. **Turn sharply left to pass a pub and reach the A53 again. Turn left again towards Buxton.**

The main road passes close to the Ramshaw Rocks, the final outlier of gritstone. Beyond the Winking Man pub the main road runs along Axe Edge, giving magnificent views, before it joins the road from Congleton and descends into Buxton.

WIRKSWORTH AND THE AMBER VALLEY FROM MATLOCK

START AND FINISH AT MATLOCK
42 MILES - 2 HOURS

The industrial heritage of Derbyshire is very obvious between Matlock and Wirksworth. Arkwright's two mills at Cromford can be seen before the road climbs past stone quarries to Wirksworth, a town which once thrived from lead mining. The route later goes through quiet countryside to follow the courses of the rivers Ecclesbourne and Amber before returning to Matlock across high moors.

Take the A6 southwards out of Matlock heading for Derby. Drive through Matlock Bath with its numerous attractions including the cable-car ride up to the Heights of Abraham, Gulliver's Kingdom Theme Park, the Peak District Mining Museum and the famous illuminated gardens. Pass the enormous Masson Mill which was built by Arkwright in 1783 and greatly enlarged in 1928, **and turn right into Cromford on to the A5012 to Newhaven and Wirksworth.** However, if you wish to make a visit to Arkwright's Cromford Mill take the road which forks left here.

Keep ahead A at the

village centre on the B5036 to Wirksworth. The Black Rock picnic area is to the left as you climb the hill out of Cromford and there are waymarked woodland walks from here. The B5035, which leaves the route to the right, goes to the National Stone Centre and Middleton Top Visitor Centre. Both places give access to the High Peak Trail.

Keep on the B5023 to go straight through Wirksworth, following signs to Duffield. This road wanders through delightful countryside, and you are left to wonder at the origins of the name of Idridgehay, especially as it is called 'Ithersee' by locals.

From here the road follows the valley of the little River Ecclesbourne, which joins with the Derwent at Duffield. The road crosses the A517 at traffic lights by the Railway Inn and soon reaches Duffield. **Turn left off the main road to the village centre and then left again B to head northwards when you meet the A6.**

Very little remains of Duffield's castle but you may visit the site. Look for steps leading up from the A6 just after a road named Castle Hill on the left. The castle was the third largest in the kingdom in Norman times, after the White Tower (part of the Tower of London) and Colchester castle. The foundations of the keep may still be seen and a stone dome covers its well.

From Duffield drive northwards on the A6 to reach Milford. In 1777 Jedediah Strutt bought the site of an old forge which stood by the bridge at Milford, at that time a hamlet of eight houses. By 1782 the mill was operational and after this the village continued to grow, in tandem with Belper where the Strutts also had mills powered by the waters of the River Derwent. With the Arkwright family, the

The Pavilion, Matlock Bath

Strutts dominated the cotton-spinning industry in Derbyshire until its decline early in the twentieth century. Unhappily none of the mills at Milford have survived.

Continue on the A6 to Belper, where the North Mill is the only survivor of the five built in the town by Jedediah Strutt and his son William. **Turn right** **C** **before reaching the middle of the town on to the Ilkeston road (A609) which is also signposted to Heage.** Go straight over at traffic lights and pass attractive cottages on the right with finely carved weatherboards. **After the White Swan fork left to Heage on the B6013 to pass the church at Belper.**

About 2 miles from Belper you come to the White Hart Inn at Heage where the famous tower windmill, the only one in the county still to have its six sails and machinery, is to the left and can be reached by footpath. **Continue on the B6013, heading for Higham and Ripley. Turn right and then left to cross the A610. Pass a lovely little gatehouse to Wingfield Park on the left and then fork left to keep on the main road (B6013) towards Higham when the Pentrich road (B6016) leaves to the right at the Devonshire Arms.** The road runs northwards up the Amber valley giving pleasant views over the river and railway line to the left. **Keep on the B6013 when it joins with the A615 for a short distance after Oakerthorpe (the road now following the ancient line of Ryknild Street).**

Continue on the B6013 past the Amber Hotel. On the other side of the road the buildings known as Toadhole Furnace commemorate bygone industrial activity and incorporate a former Friends' Meeting House dedicated in 1743. There are more lovely views as the road approaches the adjacent villages

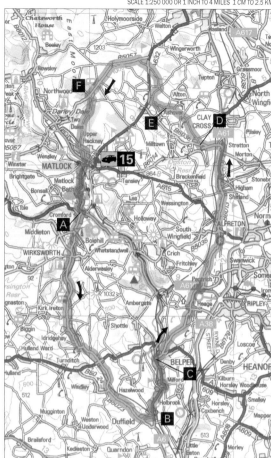

of Shirland and Higham. **Just beyond the latter village the B6013 joins with the A61, heading for Chesterfield.**

Continue travelling northwards on this road for another 2 miles until, at Stretton, it is crossed by the B6014 at the Turbutt Arms. **Turn left here towards Tansley to pass an old tollhouse. After crossing a bridge the road divides. Fork right on to the B6036 following the sign to Ashover. At the crossroads which follows** **D** **turn right to Handley.** This turn might easily be missed and comes just before the main road begins to drop down. **Go straight over the next crossroads (in the middle of tiny Handley) on to Woodhead Lane.** This is a quiet and narrow byway giving fine

views. **At a main road bear left to Littlemoor and then at a staggered crossroads keep ahead following the sign to Stone Edge.** This lane climbs up steeply between banks giving it a very ancient feel and joins another road just outside Littlemoor.

Turn right, still heading for Stone Edge. Keep on the major road when a lane, unsuitable for heavy vehicles, goes off ahead. There are extensive views from this point, nearly 1,000 feet high and known as Farhill. There are footpaths on both sides and a parking place. A little further on a view is revealed to the left over Ashover as you approach a crossroads. The main road drops down into this beautiful village **but the route bears slightly right** **E** **on an unsignposted road labelled as being**

71

Matlock History

The present town grew from Old Matlock, the village on the east bank of the River Derwent surrounding the medieval parish church and bridge. In 1698 a lead-lined wooden bath was built to catch the mineral-rich waters of a warm spring which surfaced at Matlock Bath and a hotel, the Old Bath, was built next to it. This was the beginning of Matlock as a spa town, and many more springs were developed subsequently, especially in the early nineteenth century when it became a fashionable inland resort. A new road improved access from the south at this time and several more hotels were established, one of them the New Bath where Ruskin stayed in 1829. Gradually the dale filled up with houses, hotels and 'hydropathic establishments' to join Matlock Bath with the original village. The largest of the hydros was the one put up by John Smedley in the 1850s at Matlock Bank which today serves as council offices. Smedley was a hosiery manufacturer who also built Riber Castle, now a dramatic ruin overlooking Matlock from the south-east. The town remains popular with visitors who enjoy walking through its riverside gardens and exploring the roads and footpaths which lead up the sides of the wooded dale. Cable cars are the easy way of reaching the Heights of Abraham on the western side where Victoria Tower is a wonderful viewpoint. On Sundays hundreds of bikers throng Matlock Dale, admiring each other's machines and swapping gossip.

Wirksworth

There may be mixed feelings about the town failing to attract the numbers of tourists that flock to Ashbourne or Bakewell. An exploration of Wirksworth shows it to be just as appealing with narrow lanes rising up from the market place lined with cottages with delightfully haphazard roof-lines. St Mary's, the parish church, is concealed in a peaceful circular close in the south-east sector of the town. A ceremony known as the Church Clipping takes place on the Sunday nearest to September 8 and seems to symbolise the parishioners' love of St Mary's. The congregation leaves the building during the service to encircle it, all holding hands. The building itself dates from the late thirteenth century and was restored by Sir George Gilbert Scott in the 1870s. The Saxon carvings displayed inside are of particular interest, especially the coffin lid on the north wall which is said to be the sarcophagus of an important local saint. There is also a charming representation of a lead miner setting off for work with a pick on his shoulder and a lunch-box in his hand. Wirksworth was probably important in Roman times for lead mining and the industry flourished in medieval times when the Barmote Court was established. It still meets twice a year in the Moot Hall, the oldest of all industrial courts, having operated since 1266. Wirksworth declined as the lead mines were worked out and in the eighteenth and nineteenth centuries textile mills were set up initially utilising water power but later steam. The Heritage Centre, itself occupying the premises of a former silk mill just off the market place, tells the story of Wirksworth through the centuries and has a working smithy, and silversmith's and cabinet-maker's workshops.

The Saxon Carving of a lead miner in Wirksworth church

unsuitable for heavy vehicles. It twists by some pretty cottages at Hilltop which must enjoy one of the best outlooks in Derbyshire.

The road more or less follows the contours of the high ground. **Keep heading towards Stone Edge and Chesterfield when a road leaves left to Ashover at a farm. At a T-junction turn right (again towards Stone Edge) and keep on the main road at the next junction even though the sign points to the left to Stone Edge and Chesterfield. At a T-junction turn left to Stone Edge and at the crossroads which quickly follows go straight over to Spitewinter and (yet again) Stone Edge. This road climbs to meet the A632 just to the north of the Spitewinter pub.**

after a crossroads. **At the next crossroads** **F** **– after ³/₄ mile and just before Sydnope Hill – turn left to Farley and Hackney. Fork right when the road divides to pass through more woodland** with the curious Sydnope Stand to the right, built as a Gothic eyecatcher and now a cottage. There are wonderful views over the Derwent valley and Darley Dale as the road descends steeply to Hackney. **When you come to a T-junction turn left on to Smedley Street. Keep ahead at a major road, still on Smedley Street to pass to the rear of Smedley's Hydro (two bridges span the street from the vast building). At a crossroads (Rutland Street) turn right** and then look right to see the striking façade of the Hydro, very different from the unprepossessing rear of the building which is now the headquarters of Derbyshire County Council. The road leads down to Matlock town centre. ■

Turn right and then immediately left off the main road to pass a radio mast on the left. The lane passes the well-preserved chimney of an old lead mine as it descends to the B5057.

Turn left towards Darley Dale along Stone Edge.

Keep on the B5057 to pass another radio mast – again on the left. After this the road runs straight and reaches woodland

---

• PLACES OF INTEREST •

Cromford

The first successful water-powered cotton spinning mill in the world was established in the village by Richard Arkwright in 1771. Why he chose Cromford as a site for the mill remains a mystery though he certainly knew the district, having frequently visited Wirksworth in his early days as a wig-maker. Cromford's natural advantages

included reliable streams to turn the water wheels. Initially he ignored the Derwent, preferring the more easily tamed waters of the Bonsall Brook which he combined with drainage water from an old lead mine brought across the road by an aqueduct. In 1776, 200 people were employed in the mill, most of them children working 12-hour shifts, day and night. In this year Arkwright began to build another mill on the site, seven storeys high, but this was destroyed by fire in 1890 while the two topmost storeys of the original mill were lost after another fire in 1930. Arkwright expanded the village as his enterprise grew. He built the Greyhound Hotel at its centre, a school and a chapel with rows of three-storey cottages, the top floor of these with wide windows to illuminate the weaving looms which made yarn from the mills into fabric. The mill pond

which is the most appealing feature of the village was also created by Arkwright to power the waterwheel of Cromford's corn mill. Cotton-spinning declined in Derbyshire before the middle of the nineteenth century, although Arkwright's Masson Mill survived to be enlarged in the twentieth century and only ended production recently. The buildings at Cromford later served as a brewery, laundry, and finally as a paint factory. Now they are owned by the Arkwright Society and are being painstakingly restored as craft units, shops, offices, etc. Working machinery is being re-installed gradually and £3 million has already been spent on the project since the Society bought the site in 1979.

Arkwright's Cromford Mill, Mill Lane. Site open daily except Christmas Day, 9.30–5. Telephone: (01629) 824297.

SUTTON SCARSDALE, STAINSBY MILL AND STEETLEY CHAPEL FROM BARLBOROUGH

START AND FINISH AT BARLBOROUGH
44 MILES – 2 HOURS

North-east Derbyshire is often considered an area ruined by coal mining and industry, but the mining has been discontinued and the landscape is being restored so that there is a great deal to enjoy here again. For instance there is little sign of the industrial wasteland that formerly spoilt the view from Sutton Scarsdale, the baroque ruin which overlooks the M1. Chesterfield would provide an alternative starting-point for this route.

Barlborough, situated by Junction 30 of the M1, makes a convenient starting-place for this tour of the north-east of the county. Barlborough church dates from c.1200 and is at the east end of the village close to the roundabout where the A619 meets the A616 from Clowne. **At this roundabout take the A619 towards Staveley and**

Chesterfield. There is a view of the old steel centre, with the site in the process of regeneration, as the road crosses the B6419 and drops down into Staveley.

At the roundabout near the church turn right on the B6053 to Eckington and immediately bear left up Hall Lane. The church dates from the thirteenth century but is

particularly interesting for the Frecheville Chapel of 1676 with its excellent monuments. The road passes land once occupied by the large steelworks – and now awaiting redevelopment – as it heads for Middle Handley. A road to Barrow Hill leaves to the left and after this it enters glorious countryside. **At the B6052 turn right towards Eckington and**

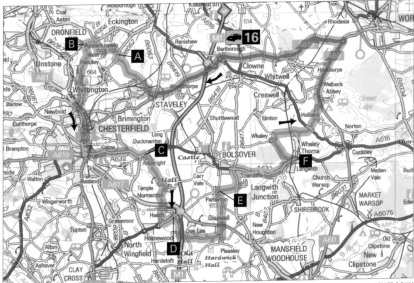

SCALE 1:250 000 OR 1 INCH TO 4 MILES *1 CM TO 2.5 KM*

then after 200 yards left **A** following the sign to Middle Handley down Westfield Lane. Bear left by the Devonshire Arms and at the next junction follow the main road to Apperknowle. At a crossroads cross straight over, again following the sign to Apperknowle. Bear left off the main road at the T-junction which follows. The top of the hill has a fine view over Dronfield.

At the T-junction by the Travellers' Rest inn at Apperknowle **B** turn left following the sign to Hundall. Keep straight on through this tiny village on to a narrow lane which climbs towards a radio mast. You might have to reverse a long way if you meet other traffic on this byway which takes you into Whittington. The road descends past the Poplar pub to pass the church on the left and reaches the main road (B6052) by the

The Revolution House, Whittington

• PLACES OF INTEREST •

Barlborough

Barlborough Hall has served as a school for many years. It was built by Sir Francis Rodes in 1583 possibly to the design of Robert Smythson as it shows the germ of many of the ideas later he used at Hardwick. Rodes was one of the judges at the trial of Mary Queen of Scots. The Hall is supposed to be haunted by a Grey Lady, the ghost of a bride who received the news of the death of her husband-to-be as she was on her way to the church. The latter dates from the twelfth century. Strangely Barlborough Old Hall has a later date than Barlborough Hall. It is large H-plan house with the year 1618 carved above the door.

Sutton Scarsdale

The ruins of the grandest mansion of its period in Derbyshire overlook the M1 as a reproach to the folly of letting such a building become derelict. The house was built for the fourth Earl of Scarsdale in 1724 to the design of Francis Smith of Warwick.

Masonry from the previous Tudor house was incorporated but completely hidden by the baroque splendour of the new house. A hint of this can be seen in the main front, but the Italian plasterwork has gone and is now in America at the Philadelphia Museum. The demolition of the back of the house reveals some Tudor brickwork. In the early twentieth century Sutton Scarsdale was owned by a descendant of Richard Arkwright, and D.H. Lawrence is said to have based the character of Sir Clifford Chatterley on this man.

The ruin is now in the care of English Heritage and the public can enjoy the grounds but are not allowed in the ruin itself.

Stainsby Mill

The mill is owned by the National Trust who have restored its machinery to illustrate the working of a nineteenth-century water-powered corn mill. There has been a mill at Stainsby since medieval times but the present one was rebuilt in 1849–50 and fitted with new machinery. The waterwheel stands 17 feet high and is made of cast iron. It is driven by water falling into its buckets just above its half-way height and is thus a 'high breast shot' wheel. It not only drives the millstones but provides power for lifting sacks, cleaning the grain, and sieving the flour after it has been ground. Visitors are able to see these operations from viewing galleries. Open April–October, Wednesdays, Thursdays, Saturdays, Sundays and Bank Holiday Mondays 12.30–4. Telephone: (01246) 850430.

Revolution House (see page 23) and the Cock and Magpie inn. **Turn right here and after about ³/₄ mile take the second exit at the roundabout on to the A61 into Chesterfield.**

Take the Bolsover road (A632) out of Chesterfield past the Royal Hospital at Calow. About 1¹/₂ miles after this you come to Arkwright Town. **Immediately after crossing a bridge over a disused railway turn right C to Sutton Scarsdale down Sutton Lane.** After about 2 miles the lane passes the drive to the grand but sadly derelict mansion on the left as it enters the village.

After visiting the hall (where the grassy surroundings offer splendid views and are good for picnics) return to the main road and turn left to head for Heath and Holmewood. This road crosses a bridge over the A617 to come to a T-junction. **Turn right and then almost immediately left following signs to Holmewood, North Wingfield and Mansfield. At the junction with the A6175 turn left and pass a turn to Heath village on the left but then turn right D to Stainsby. Take the first turning left off this road to pass under the M1 and reach Stainsby Mill.**

The drive to Hardwick Hall (see Tour 3) goes off to the right

Revolution House (see page 23)

• PLACES OF INTEREST •

Welbeck Abbey

The mansion is an army staff college and casual visitors are not encouraged though there are public footpaths through the park. In the nineteenth century the fifth Duke of Portland enlarged the already palatial mansion by building underground. He was an eccentric who disliked human contact and his staff were ordered to ignore him, communicating by means of the letterboxes in the doors of the rooms he used. He built an underground ballroom nearly 60 yards long as well as a billiard-room able to hold twelve full-sized tables. Fifteen miles of tunnels were made underneath the estate so that the Duke could move about surreptitiously. One of the tunnels, lined with glazed white bricks and leading to the station, was wide enough to take a coach-and-four!

Steetley Chapel

'The most perfect and elaborate specimen of Norman architecture to be found anywhere in Europe' is how one expert describes the tiny chapel hidden away off the A619. Quite a few art historians might have reservations about that statement but there is no denying that it is unique and of rare beauty. It lay derelict for many years in the last century before being restored in 1880 and some of the remarkable carving of the porch had to be re-done at that time. Inside, much of the Norman work survives intact – that in the apse being outstanding. No-one knows the reason why such a small building was built with such a wealth of decoration in the middle of the twelfth century. The chapel is normally locked and the best way of seeing it is probably by attending evensong.

---

opposite the mill. **Bear left on a lovely country lane which leads to Ault Hucknall.** The church is the first thing you see as you enter the village (which seems only to comprise a church and a farm). The former is architecturally important but unfortunately is usually locked. Keep on past a turn to the right and **at a T-junction turn left down Rowthorne Lane towards Glapwell. Go straight**

over the A617 on Bolsover Road and after 2 miles, at crossroads on the outskirts of Palterton, take the road to the right E to Scarcliffe. Cross over the B6417 by the Horse and Groom inn and enter the village.** Pass ivy-covered Scarcliffe Hall Farm and come to the church on the left. Note how the sun-dial has been corrected by being angled away from the wall of the tower. The church dates from Norman times and contains an outstanding monument of a woman with a child in her arms which itself dates from the twelfth or thirteenth century. The effigy probably represents Constantia de Frecheville who died in 1175. She is known in the village as the Lady Constantia and a curfew bell is tolled in her memory for the three weeks either side of Christmas.

Continue on the road through the village to come to the A632 and turn right to Nether Langwith and Cuckney. Turn left when you come to a T-junction, staying on the A632. At Nether Langwith go

Stainsby Mill

underneath the railway bridge where traffic is controlled by lights and then turn left almost immediately 🅵 **to Whaley.** However, if you wish to visit Whaley Thorns Heritage Centre take the following turn left to find the Heritage Centre which is situated in a disused school. There is a display telling the long history of coal mining in the district and the efforts being made to restore its natural landscape.

The lane to Whaley goes beneath a small viaduct and past a pond to the left. The reclaimed land to the right was once Langwith coal mine. The car park to the right is for those who wish to walk the Archaeological Way, a path which leads to Creswell Caves. **Turn right off the main road when the road divides at Whaley, and then right again at a T-junction. After the few houses at Whaley Common turn right at the next T-junction.** There are wide views from this quiet lane which soon reaches a level crossing where

Effigy of Lady Constantia in Scarcliffe church

you have to press a bell to attract the crossing-keeper's attention. The line runs from Worksop to Alfreton and is used only by goods trains. The lane comes to a junction with a main road. **Keep ahead here to the A616 (Newark to Sheffield road). Go straight across this.** You see

the trees of Welbeck Park (originally part of Sherwood Forest) ahead as you pass through Holbeck and come to the A60. **Turn left towards Worksop.**

The Dukeries Garden Centre, an Adventure Park and the Harley Gallery are immediately to the right and occupy outbuildings of Welbeck Abbey. A turning left after this (B6042) goes to Creswell Crags. Keep on the main road to enter Nottinghamshire. The imposing entrance to Worksop Manor is to the right just before a roundabout. Worksop Manor was a great house on the scale of Hardwick Hall – it was burnt down in 1761 and subsequently only partly rebuilt.

Pass through the hamlet of Darfoulds and go under a railway bridge. A straight length of road follows. At the end of this a byway to the right goes to Steetley Chapel, just inside the county limits of Derbyshire. About 1½ miles after this there is a large layby on the right of the road which is useful for walks in Whitwell Wood where there is a circular drive with seven more drives radiating from its centre. Pass the Van Dyck Hotel and a Garden Centre with a tearoom and then **cross the A618 to return to Barlborough.** ◼

Steetley Chapel

BEELEY MOOR AND THE HIGH PEAK FROM BAKEWELL

START AND FINISH AT BAKEWELL
36 MILES – 2 HOURS

It is interesting to compare the villages visited on this tour. Pilsley is a typical estate village, built by Paxton for the Duke of Devonshire, while Elton is equally typical as a village which grew up on lead mining and was left adrift when the industry ended in the eighteenth century. Sheldon is another mining village which has the Magpie Mine on its outskirts to help to illustrate what these villages must have looked like in their heyday.

Take the Baslow road (A619) northwards out of Bakewell and cross the ancient bridge over the River Wye. Turn right immediately after the bridge and climb the hill, bearing right on to a road which is unsuitable for lorries. This road climbs steeply to cross an old railway bridge by the former site of Bakewell station. Bakewell was on the Midland Railway's line between Manchester and Derby via Buxton and in 1922 had seven stopping trains on weekdays in each direction. The trackbed is now used by the Monsal Trail. The road climbs past the golf course giving grand views. Care is needed on a hairpin bend as the road goes through the northern end of Manners Wood. At the top of the hill there are wonderful views ahead. This is a favourite road with picnickers and there are several places to park.

At a T-junction turn right on to the B6048. Pilsley is on the right, a village of estate cottages designed by Paxton which should not be confused with the place with the same name near Clay Cross. Chatsworth Farm Shop is to the right. **Turn left when you reach the B6012 to drive through Chatsworth**

The River Wye at Bakewell

All Saints' Church, Bakewell

You have to climb to the church from the centre of the town but the effort is worthwhile for it is interesting historically as well as architecturally. The spire and octagonal tower are Victorian and replaced medieval ones which rose 16 feet higher. The Vernon Chapel in the east aisle of the south transept contains the fascinating memorials to the owners of Haddon Hall. The one mounted on the north wall is to Sir John Manners and his wife Dorothy

whose famous elopement is the most romantic of all Peakland tales. The one facing it on the south wall is to Sir George Manners, who died in 1623, and his wife. Their nine children are shown below, a baby in swaddling clothes wearing a malign expression which stays with you long after you have left the church.

Darley Dale

St Helen's church is a twelfth-thirteenth century cruciform church with two fine windows designed by Burne-Jones, an interesting medieval monument to Sir John de Darley and a peal of eight bells, dating from 1618. The churchyard has one of the largest yew trees in England with a circumference of 33 feet at four feet from the ground.

Winster

A hundred or so years ago Winster would certainly have been called a town, with a market being held in the arcade beneath the Market House and probably spilling out into the narrow street. The building dates from medieval times but was rebuilt in the late seventeenth or early eighteenth century and now serves as a National Trust information centre. Today Winster has the character of a village, albeit a beautiful and self-sufficient one that still has shops and a pub. It has many exceptional houses dating from the late seventeenth century and Georgian times. Winster Hall, set back from the main street, is a particularly fine example of an early-Georgian town house. The tower of Winster's church dates from this era but the rest is nineteenth century and uses an original, successful idea to integrate twin aisles with the chancel. Like Darley Dale, it has glass by Burne-Jones and also an unusual font.

Park, heading for Baslow. Turn right on to the Chesterfield road (A619) at the roundabout after the bridge at Baslow and then right again at the following roundabout after the village, still on the A619. After 3 miles the road reaches the **Highwayman pub at Eastmoor and $1/2$ mile after this take the turning right at crossroads A signposted to Beeley.**

Keep on this very pleasant country road for about 2 miles, ignoring the numerous turnings which leave it. There are wide views to the left towards Chesterfield and heather-covered moors to the right with grouse butts. **At a T-junction turn right, still following the sign to Beeley and Darley Dale.** There is woodland to the left after

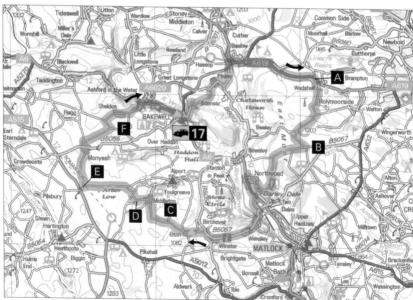

SCALE 1:250 000 OR 1 INCH TO 4 MILES *1 CM TO 2.5 KM*

this as the road climbs to cross a high area of bog – to the right this is called Hipper Sick while Umbersley Sick is further to the north-west. **At the next T-junction turn left (where the signpost is currently broken) and in about ¹/₂ mile turn very sharply right B towards Rowsley.** The road crosses the southern end of East Moor and gives more wide views across heather-covered moors. **About 1¹/₂ miles after the sharp turn, and near the end of a straight length of road, there is a concealed and unsignposted turning to the left. Take this turn on to a bumpy lane which appropriately passes a house called Bumper Castle.** Wooded

Hall Dale is to the left. The lane gradually descends into Darley Dale through woodland. **Keep bearing right to follow the lane down to reach the A6.**

Turn left on to this and follow it for about a mile before taking the first turning to the right to Darley Dale parish church. Predictably this is Church Lane but is better known to locals as Ghost Lane because a pedlar was murdered by the church in the seventeenth century and his ghost haunts here. It crosses the Peak Railway at a level crossing and passes the beautiful church to reach the B5057. **Turn right to cross Darley Bridge over the River Derwent** (there is a camp site and picnic centre on the right just

before the bridge). **The B5057 goes through Wensley and then follows Wensley Dale to Winster. Go straight through the beautiful little town with its old market hall and many fine buildings of similar age, heading for Elton.**

At the junction with the B5056 go straight over to Elton. The tiny village has a youth hostel, pub, teashop and a church, the latter dating from 1812. Pass the church and keep ahead to descend the hill into the natural amphitheatre of Gratton Dale. This is lovely countryside criss-crossed with footpaths. **Just beyond Dale End the road divides with a long building to the left which was once a cheese factory. Take the lane to the left C** which climbs to pass the site of Smerrill, a village abandoned in medieval times, perhaps because of the Black Death. This enchanting lane gives wonderful views as you descend with an almost canyon-like dale to the right with much exposed rock. It passes beautiful Smerrill Grange and comes to Middleton-by-Youlgreave.

Turn left in the village centre following the sign towards Newhaven and Ashbourne. The lane climbs beneath tall trees to come to a

The Peak Railway, Darley Dale

Monyash

Geology accounts for the position of the village high on the plateau of the White Peak. It is situated at a point where a small bed of clay lies on the limestone giving rise to springs which originally fed five meres. Only one of these survives, surrounded by a wall to keep animals away from the precious supply of drinking water. Monyash once had a busy market, receiving the charter for this in 1340, and the market cross of this time still stands on the green. The tiny Friends' Meeting House, dating from 1711, is all that is left to show that Monyash was a thriving centre for Quakerism and John Bright used the village as a summer retreat in the nineteenth century. The beautiful church has transepts, tower and spire like Bakewell and dates from 1198. It was enthusiastically restored by Butterfield in 1884 though it has to be admitted that the woodwork he supplied is excellent. The enormous parish chest is probably as old as the church itself.

Magpie Mine

The shaft of the mine is more than 700 feet deep and the sough, or drainage tunnel, was 1¼ miles long until it collapsed after the mine had been finally abandoned in 1958. After this, water pressure built up within the hill and was only released by a water explosion in 1966 which blew a crater in the hillside. The mine was always an unlucky one, its boom years coming when the price of lead was low after vast sums had been spent on improving it. In 1872 the Magpie Mine was the third greatest producer of lead ore in Derbyshire and was rapidly recouping the capital spent on drainage. In 1885 the world market was swamped by cheap ore from Australia, and though the mine struggled on sporadically until the 1950s it was never profitable. The engine house dates from 1864 and was built to shelter a 70-inch Cornish engine which was originally installed to raise water 700 feet to the surface. This it failed to do and the sough was driven through from the River Wye to provide more efficient drainage. It took eight years to cut and by the time it was completed in 1881 the price of lead was beginning to fall.

junction near the end of the belt of trees. **Turn right**  **here to Monyash and cross straight over a major road which follows,** joining the White Peak Scenic Route and continuing to head for Monyash. **At an** **unsignposted T-junction bear left on to a major road** which is known as Long Rake after the innumerable open-cast lead workings which litter the landscape. The road passes the driveway to Arbor Low to the left

(see page 29) **and then turn right at a main road**  **to Monyash,** still following the Scenic Route sign.

You can soon see the spire of Monyash church as the road descends to pass the village pond. Go straight over the B5055 into the village which is built on a hill. **On the far side of the village take the turn to the right to Sheldon.** This road has an ancient feel to it – a fairly straight, wide-verged thoroughfare running between stone walls. **Turn left to Sheldon at a T-junction**  **where the chimney and engine house of the Magpie Mine face you and after ¾ mile bear right into the village when the main road goes left.** This is a lovely quiet little village with a broad street with sycamores shading it. The Victorian church is to the left. As you leave Sheldon there is a fine view to the left as you descend into Kirk Dale. **Turn left when you reach a main road towards Ashford in the Water. This soon takes you to the A6 – turn right. Ashford village is to the left. Keep on the main road to reach Bakewell.** ■

![Winster Market House]

Winster Market House

ECCLES PIKE, BUXTON AND THE WHITE PEAK FROM CASTLETON

47 MILES – 2½ HOURS
START AND FINISH AT CASTLETON

The drive will take you to many of the best-known places in the Peak District and to some which are much less famous but hardly less attractive. You will meet only a handful of people who know the whereabouts of Foolow or Abney yet these villages are set amongst particularly beautiful countryside. Castleton, with its caves and castle, is an attractive village and an excellent starting point for exploring the area.

Take the A625 westwards out of Castleton. After 1½ miles the road ahead via Mam Tor is permanently closed having been blocked by a landslide in 1977. **Cars are now diverted to the left to climb through Winnats**

Pass past the entrance to Speedwell Cavern. The crags to the left overlooking the pass resemble fairy-tale castles and in early summer the green of the grass here is startling against the white of the exposed limestone.

Turn right at the major road (B6061) at the top of the pass to Chapel-en-le-Frith. Blue John Cave is to the right as the former main road is rejoined. A little way further and the road to Edale leaves to the right. **Keep on the main road (now the A625) which gives continuously changing views of the limestone countryside as it traverses Rushup Edge.** As the road begins to descend, the entrance to the Chestnut Centre is to the right **and about ¾ mile further on cross beneath the Chapel-en-le-Frith bypass and turn right on to the B5470 to reach the town centre.**

Keep ahead on the B5470 through the town to take a turn to the right A to Whitehough and Chinley (which comes just before the 50 mph speed limit starts). This is Crossings Road which passes by modern housing and an enclosure on the right surrounding 'Nanny's Well', a medicinal spring of mineral-rich water. **Leave Crossings Road by taking the first turn to the left,** by a pretty row of cottages, following a sign towards Eccles Pike and Hilltop. The lane is crossed by several footpaths and

Castleton

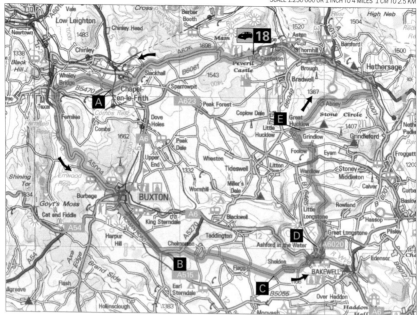

passes a beautiful farm to the right before reaching the car park for Eccles Pike. A short climb takes you up to this brilliant viewpoint. On a clear day you can look north to spot traffic on the A624 near Chinley Head at least three miles away. To the south the view extends over Cockyard

Reservoir to Combs Edge.

The lane descends to the main road, swinging left after a farm and passing some lovely houses. **Cross straight over the B5470 on to Elnor Lane.** This is a tricky turn, right and then acutely left. **When the houses end the lane narrows and divides.**

Keep ahead on the major road here, an attractive lane which passes a Methodist chapel, unusual in having a graveyard – this one with a fine outlook over the Goyt Valley. **The road descends to the A5004 to Buxton where you turn left.** This main road gives more fine

---

• *PLACES OF INTEREST* •

Castleton

There may have been a small settlement of lead miners here when William Peverel built the first castle in 1086 but it seems unlikely. Peverel was a trusted lieutenant of the Conqueror (and possibly his bastard son) who was made bailiff of the lead-producing lands of north Derbyshire. The castle was built to protect these interests on a superb natural site, with precipitous slopes to east, west and much of the south, and a steep one to the north. Castleton grew up below the castle to a plan drawn up by its Norman overlord. The castle reverted to the monarch after two generations of Peverel rule and in 1157 was chosen by Henry II as the place where he accepted the surrender of Malcolm II of Scotland. In 1176

Henry decided to rebuild the stronghold and most of what we see today dates from this time. Interior and exterior walls were faced with ashlar but most of this dressed stone was removed as the castle became steadily more ruinous after Edward III's visit in 1331. He gave it to his son (John of Gaunt, Duke of Lancaster) and Peverel Castle remains the property of the Duchy of Lancaster to this day, though it is cared for by English Heritage. Sir Walter Scott wrote a romantic novel about the Peverel family (*Peveril of the Peak*) and this may be the reason for the difference in spelling. Castleton church was also Norman but was drastically restored in 1837. Surprisingly the seventeenth-century box pews survived. On Oak Apple Day (29

May or 28 May if it falls on a Sunday) crowds throng to the village for Garland Day, a ceremony which may have pagan roots but is more likely to have started as a celebration for the restoration of Charles II. A horseman in Stuart costume wears a three-foot high garland which hides the top half of his body. Beginning at one of Castleton's pubs (they take it in turn) he leads a procession around the town which ends at the church where the garland is hauled to the top of the tower and fixed to a pinnacle. The band plays a special 'Garland Tune' which is strikingly similar to that of the Cornish Floral Dance and probably shows the influence of the Cornish miners who came southwards when the West Country tin deposits were worked out.

The view from Eccles Pike

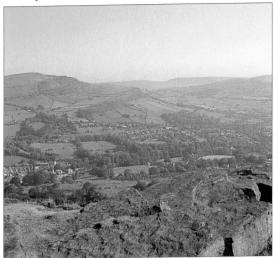

views before it descends Long Hill into the spa town.

From the town centre take the A515 towards Ashbourne. Follow this main road for about 3 miles (its straightness testifies to its being a Roman road). **Just after the B5053 goes to the right to Longnor take the road left (A5270) towards Bakewell. A mile further on fork right B to Chelmorton.** Keep on the main road when a lane to the left goes to the village, which makes a pretty picture from this top road. The church spire can be seen nestling in the trees in the distance. It is unusual for its row of dormer windows. The church is a puzzling mixture of styles from c.1200 – c.1500. Keep on the main road as a lane leaves to the left to Taddington and then another to the right to Flagg. This is a top-of-the-world road and you can see for miles as it runs for several miles, fairly straight and wide. Eventually the engine house and chimney of a lead mine come into view – this is the Magpie Mine, which has a colourful history and is the best-preserved eighteenth/ nineteenth-century lead mine in the country. **Turn left off the main road C when the latter swings right, following the signpost to Sheldon.**

After passing through Sheldon the road meets another at a T-junction in Kirk Dale. **Turn left towards Bakewell and descend to the A6. Turn right on to this and then left on the A6020 into Ashford in the Water. Cross the bridge, take the first turning on the left (B6465) and then the first right opposite the Ashford Hotel on to the B6465 following the sign to Monsal Head and Wardlow. After about ½ mile, at a crossroads, take the first turning to the right off this road D on an unsignposted lane (sign damaged) which has a notice saying it is unsuitable for heavy goods vehicles.** This is Shady Lane

which gets its name from a ghostly procession of twelve headless men bearing a coffin. The haunting forewarns death and the coffin is supposed to be empty – but how would anyone know? Nevertheless this is a pleasant lane which leads through a leafy dale where there are grand entrances on each side of the road. The one to the right is to Thornbridge Hall, a Georgian house extravagantly rebuilt in neo-Tudor style in 1871 (not open).

At Great Longstone a medieval cross is at the centre of the village. Turn left here to pass the Crispin Inn and the gates to Longstone Hall on the right. The house dates from 1747 and you can see its stately red-brick façade. **After this, turn right off the main road up Moor Road heading towards Longstone Edge.** There is dramatic limestone scenery as the lane climbs steeply and crosses a cattle-grid to reach the top of High Rake where there are plenty of picnic places but little in the way of shelter if the wind is blowing. **Keep on the main road across the Longstone Moor, bearing right at a T-junction to reach the A623.**

Turn right on to the main road but leave it in about 200 yards by turning left to follow the sign to Foolow. Turn left again at a T-junction to come to another T-junction by the Bull's Head inn at Foolow.

Magpie Mine, Sheldon

Turn left and keep on the main road to pass the memorably-named Silly Dale on the left and a lane to Grindlow on the right. Continue to the next major junction to take the road on the right into Great Hucklow. Turn right at a T-junction in the middle of the village – the pub is to the left.

The road climbs through trees and there are views across the wide plain known as Shepherd's Flat. **After ½ mile take the road to the left** ◼ **(an acute turn, this) to continue to follow the sign to the Gliding Club.** The lane leads up Hucklow Edge to the airfield at the top. There are magnificent views from here as well as a viewing enclosure for those who like to watch the gliders being towed into the air. **Keep to the upper road until the road divides to drop to the straggling village of Abney.** The road dips down into a conifer plantation and an inviting-looking footpath goes off to the left to Bradwell. Highlow Hall is to the right, a fifteenth-century manor house which once belonged to the Eyre family and has the reputation of being the most haunted house in Derbyshire. Just beyond the hall a wonderful view is revealed over the Hope Valley with Hathersage church an eyecatcher. **The lane comes to the B6001 at the Cow Inn. Turn left into Hathersage.**

Gliding at Great Hucklow

• PLACES OF INTEREST •

Ashford in the Water

Like Castleton, this village also had a garland ceremony but one without jollity. When a young girl died in the village a garland of paper rosettes known as a virgin crant would be made and carried before the coffin at the funeral. They would then be hung in the church where four of them may still be seen, the oldest dating from 1747. The Norman and medieval church was rebuilt in 1868 though the original tympanum was saved. Sheepwash Bridge, the medieval packhorse bridge close to the church, is now just a footbridge. It got its name as the River Wye was used for washing sheep at this point before they were sheared. Lambs would be penned into the stone enclosure on the south side of the river and their mothers thrown in from the opposite bank. They would naturally swim across the river in response to the plaintive cries of their offspring. Ashford has six wells which are dressed for Trinity Sunday and this attracts many thousands of visitors to the village.

Derbyshire Well-Dressing

The origins of this famous ceremony may be pagan but it is known that wells were dressed at Tissington in 1615 after a severe drought throughout which they continued to flow. A wooden frame is covered in puddled clay and a paper covering bearing the design fixed over it. The design is pricked through on to the clay and background colours filled in with mosses, bark, fir-cones, etc. After this, the laborious process of fixing petals is begun to make the main part of the display, each petal overlapping to allow rainwater to drain off. The themes are usually biblical but may illustrate local or topical subjects. Well-dressing has spread to many other parts of the country in recent years but had its origins in the Peak District where some villages, like Ashford, decorate several wells.

This road meets the A625 opposite the George Hotel. **Turn left to pass Bamford where the road to the Derwent Reservoirs leaves to the right (A6013). Keep ahead here and drive another 2½ miles to reach Hope, a village dominated by the large cement works. Turn left immediately after the church, opposite the Woodroffe Arms Hotel, following a signpost to 'Cement Works'.** Ignore the turn to Bradwell to the left and keep on the road which climbs steadily to Pindale. Beware of meeting cement lorries – do not become distracted by the fine views, with Peveril Castle easily identifiable ahead. After the works the road becomes narrow and passes Pindale Farm on the left where you can see the former engine house and chimney of the Pindale lead mine. The views over the Hope Valley grow even more impressive as you near Castleton. The way is narrow and sufferers from vertigo might find little pleasure in it at times. It goes through woods before meeting another lane on the outskirts of Castleton. This leads through a little square and passes the church before ending at the A625 in the middle of the village. The car park is just to the right. ◼

HATHERSAGE AND THE DARK PEAK FROM GLOSSOP

61 MILES – 2½ HOURS
START AND FINISH AT GLOSSOP

A road known as the Snake must have romance attached to it, especially when it threads its way through some of England's finest highland country. The route leaves the A57 to skirt the moorland on the edge of Sheffield and drop to Hathersage, a village with connections with both Little John and Charlotte Brontë. The return is through Chapel-en-le-Frith and Hayfield. The latter is one of the loveliest villages of the Dark Peak, where the mass trespass of Kinder Scout began in 1932.

Take the A57 out of Glossop heading for Sheffield. The parish church is at Old Glossop, off to the left from this road about a mile from the town centre. On leaving the town the main road climbs steadily from the Royal Oak pub, where horses used to be changed for the long climb which lay ahead to the Snake Inn. If you were walking up the hill you would keep a sharp lookout about a mile after Royal Oak for the letters 'M.M.H.' chiselled in the wall. They stand for 'Man Murdered Here' and commemorate the murder, in 1838, of an unknown man who left the pub after foolishly boasting of the fortune he had made that day at market.

The summit of the Snake Pass is reached 4½ miles from Glossop at a height of 1,680 feet. The roadside parking places near the crest are popular with people walking on the Pennine Way which crosses the road at the summit. The former packhorse route – Doctor's Gate – is to the north of the main road. This dates from Roman times but was reconstructed in the sixteenth century. Beyond Doctor's Gate the road zigzags through Lady Clough, the spectacular gorge which gave the Snake Pass Inn its original name (Lady Clough Inn). The Snake Pass takes its name from

• PLACES OF INTEREST •

Hathersage
The name of the village is supposed to come from 'Heather's Edge' but there may be an older and less appropriate derivation. Hathersage stands at the point where the limestone of the White Peak meets the gritstone of the Dark Peak, and at a quarry on the Longshaw estate there are dozens of millstones abandoned when the need for them declined in the 1920s. This ended one of the industries of the village and came after many others had faded. There were five smoky mills which made needles, pins, and fine-drawn wire in the nineteenth century but none of these lasted for long in the twentieth. The church occupies a striking position on the flank of a

small hill and is famous for the grave of Little John (page 51). It

dates from 1381 but was restored by Butterfield in 1849–52. Its most interesting features are the

fifteenth- and sixteenth-century tombs and brasses of members of the Eyre family. Charlotte Brontë was the schoolfriend of the sister of the vicar of Hathersage and probably took the name of Eyre for her heroine from these memorials. She also took Hathersage as a model for her 'Morton' in the book – she stayed at the George and the landlord of the day was Mr Morton. Scattered around Hathersage are seven old halls all of which were supposed to have been built by Robert Eyre (who died in 1459) for each of his seven sons. Robert lived at Highlow Hall, the most haunted house in Derbyshire and two other former Eyre homes, North Lees and Moorseats, also have ghosts.

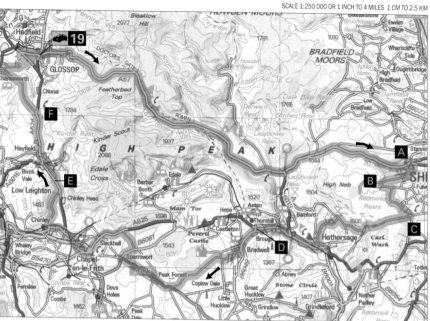

the crest of the Duke of Devonshire who was chairman of the Turnpike Trust which built the road. The crest shows a snake and the inn soon adopted the emblem and thus gave a name to the road. The surface was of loosely compacted limestone until the 1930s when it was first sprayed with tar. The Snake Inn (it became the Snake Pass Inn much later) used to be popular with shooters of grouse and was taken over by shooting parties after the Glorious Twelfth, the man shooting the most birds sitting at the head of the table. Because of its remote location prize-fights once took place in the meadows below the inn.

The road follows the valley of the River Ashop. The woods of the valley used to be rich in alder trees and the seasoned wood was taken to Lancashire to be made into clogs. In 1836 a flash flood swept away two foresters with their horse. Their bodies were taken downriver for 10 miles, eventually being found at Grindleford. Nowadays the Ashop flows through the Woodlands Valley and into the Ladybower Reservoir. The track on the far side of the valley is part of the

Roman road from Yorkshire Bridge and Bamford which follows the turnpike way to Glossop, though often at a distance.

About 2 miles beyond the Snake Pass Inn the road crosses a bridge over the little River Alport. A track follows the valley from here up to Alport Castles Farm. John Wesley used to preach in a barn here and attracted large congregations. On the first Sunday in July the barn is used for a service called a Lovefeast, which

commemorates the persecution of non-conformists when people had to worship secretly in remote locations like this. Alport Castles are dramatic gritstone towers which were formed by a massive landslip which occurred quite recently in the timescale of geology.

The road to the Derwent and Howden reservoirs is to the left just before the A6013 goes to the right to Bamford and Hathersage. **Stay on the A57 to cross Cutthroat Bridge as the road**

Old Glossop

Abandoned millstones, Stanage Edge

climbs up Hordron Edge. Not surprisingly the name was given to the bridge after a gruesome incident in the late sixteenth century when a man from Wormhill was set upon by footpads. There is a road on the left to Strines just after this and then after a further 4 miles the road divides, the A6101 going to the left down the Rivelin Valley.

Keep on the A57 here but after 300 yards turn right **A** on to Lodge Lane on a road with a 3-ton weight limit. This is a steep climb with zigzag bends. At a crossroads turn right to pass a golf course and the Sportsman pub. At the next junction **B** the road ahead is a dead end leading to the Redmire Reservoirs where there are car parks for sightseers, picnickers and walkers. To continue the tour turn left at this junction and then right at the next turn opposite a sign to Brownhills Lane. This is Brown Edge, a ridge giving a comprehensive view of Sheffield to the east. Keep on the main road to come to Ringinglow Road **C** and turn right.

The road turns its back on Sheffield, striking westwards back into Derbyshire across Burbage Moor where Yorkshire is to the left and Derbyshire to the right. It is another area of wild moorland popular with walkers. The road dips down to cross a deep valley with Burbage Rocks to the left and Stanage Edge to the right. **Bear right when the road divides, ignore a turn to the right to Ladybower, and keep on to Hathersage.** A view of the Hope Valley opens up to the right as the road begins its descent to Hathersage. **At the A625 turn right into the village.**

Keep on the A625 out of Hathersage and pass the turn to Bamford (A6013). 2 miles beyond this junction, opposite The Travellers pub, turn left **D** off the A625 on to the B6049 to Bradwell. The hamlet of Brough at this turning was the site of Navio, a Roman fort established c.75 AD which probably existed for nearly three hundred years and, like the later Peveril Castle, was designed to protect the lead and silver mines of the district.

A mile or so further on Bradwell is a cheerful village of haphazardly arranged cottages which grew around lead mining

---

• PLACES OF INTEREST •

Chinley
The two railway viaducts at Chinley were described by Henry Thorold as one of the greatest monuments to Victorian industrial England: 'To the motorist or pedestrian passing underneath the effect of them is crushing, breath-taking.' The twin viaducts joined near Chinley station, which was an important junction for the Manchester to London line with trains from Sheffield joining it from the east. The station had five waiting-rooms, a bookstall and a refreshment room. If you have an interest in industrial history it is worth the short detour to Buxworth, which lies a mile to the west. Here there is a well-preserved canal basin built for the Peak Forest Canal in 1800, with the remains of a tramway of the same time which was designed to bring gritstone and limestone to the canal terminus. Buxworth was previously named Buggsworth, but the villagers got tired of being ridiculed and changed the name of their village.

Hayfield
There is the feeling of a holiday resort about Hayfield on a good summer weekend, with its shops and pubs crowded and walkers setting off for Kinder Scout or Ashop Head. The mass trespass of Kinder Scout in 1932 began from Hayfield and the idea of a National Park grew from this demonstration for walkers' rights. After two tragic accidents involving lorries careering down the steep hill into the village, a bypass now leaves Hayfield at peace, though it may be confusing to motorists to discover that the only way back to the main road is from the south end of the village. In former towns several mills utilised the waters of the River Sett which surge powerfully down from Kinder Scout after heavy rain. One flash flood carried the cricket club's heavy roller three miles downstream, all the way to New Mills.

and smelting. Silk and cotton-spinning were cottage industries at the same time. Millinery and hat-making developed and at one time there were seven hatters working in Bradwell. Samuel Fox, the inventor of the folding umbrella, was born in the village in 1815. He also founded Stockwell steelworks and was a great local benefactor.

Go through Bradwell on the main road, passing the Victorian church on the left, and then turn right at the end of the village down Dale End to double back for a short way before turning left up Towngate to pass the White Hart inn and come to a crossroads. Go straight over here and climb out of the village past a large quarry to reach a junction at the top of the hill. Turn right to pass another quarry entrance and then, after 200 yards, turn left on to a lane which has a weight restriction. This goes past the remains of the Rake Mine where the road passes through quarry workings. Beyond is a pleasant lane which gives wide views. However, there are several sharp bends on this road so care is needed before it reaches the A623. **Turn right towards Peak**

Forest and Sparrowpit. Peak Forest was famous for its Gretna-style marriages in the past (see page 45).

At the Wanted Inn at Sparrowpit (see page 44) turn right on to the road to Edale (B6061). After about 3/4 mile, as the road dips down to a pond, turn left on to a lane with a 7 1/2-ton weight restriction. This pleasant byway follows a dry valley before climbing up to the A625. The battlemented tower on the skyline is a ventilation shaft of the Cowburn railway tunnel. **Turn left on to the A625 towards Chapel-en-le-Frith.** There are fine views as you descend into the town. Pass the entrance to the Chestnut Centre (see page 47) on the right, **go beneath the bypass and then turn right to follow the signs towards Chapel-en-le-Frith town centre and Whaley Bridge. After 200 yards take the turning right into Hayfield Road following the sign to Glossop (A624). This road takes you past the Ferodo works to a roundabout. Carry straight on here, still on the A624 but now following signs to Chinley and Hayfield to go under the bypass again.** At

Chapel Milton the road passes below twin viaducts. The place is named after the unusual independent chapel of 1711, long and narrow and built of stone. **Bear left on the B6062 when the Glossop road goes right. Continue for another mile but then turn sharp right opposite the Squirrels Hotel in Chinley to cross a railway bridge and turn right up Maynestone Road.** This climbs up past houses which enjoy wide-ranging views over an unspoilt landscape. This road eventually rejoins the A624 after about 2 miles. **Turn left and then after 300 yards it is worth taking Highgate Road, the unobtrusive turning to the right E.** This is a loop road into Hayfield which provides a choice of excellent picnic places as well as a succession of fine views and choice of footpaths.

At Hayfield the route continues by turning left before the centre of the attractive village and the church to reach the A624 which bypasses Hayfield. Turn right on to the main road which goes through Little Hayfield and then climbs steadily. Look for a turn to the left F as it twists and turns to reach the summit. Take this road, signposted to Charlesworth and known as the Monk's Road, which gives views to the north-east over Glossop and the moors beyond the town. It climbs to reach a summit where there is a car park allowing motorists to pause to enjoy the scenery. Westwards the view extends over Greater Manchester towards Merseyside. The road descends by the high wall of a cemetery into Charlesworth. **At a T-junction turn right to Simmondley and Glossop.** Follow this lane past the Hare and Hounds and through new housing to come to a mini-roundabout on the A57. **Take the second exit to reach Glossop town centre.** ■

An otter at the Chestnut Centre

ASHBY-DE-LA-ZOUCH, THE TRENT VALLEY AND SOUTH-EAST DERBYSHIRE FROM MELBOURNE

START AND FINISH AT MELBOURNE
54 MILES – 2½ HOURS

Although the scenery on this tour may lack the spectacular features of limestone country, quiet lanes lead to delightful towns and villages which have often had eventful pasts. The tour starts from the inviting town of Melbourne and takes you through Erewash, the district between Derby and Nottingham which is often mistakenly dismissed as being flat and without interest.

Take the B587 Ashby road out of Melbourne which is later signposted to Coleorton. Pass a turn to the right to Staunton Harold Reservoir where there are picnic places, walks and fishing. About a mile from Melbourne you enter Leicestershire and after a road leaves to the left to Breedon on the Hill another goes to the right to Calke, Smisby and Staunton Harold. Keep ahead on the B587 to pass the main entrance to Staunton Harold Hall on the right (see page 40). The classic view of the mansion and church by the lakeside can be seen just after the driveway.

At a T-junction about a mile further on turn right to pass through Lount, join the A50 at a roundabout and so come to Ashby-de-la-Zouch. Turn left off the main street to see the castle, otherwise follow it to a mini-roundabout and turn right, going towards Burton upon Trent on the A50.

After 1 mile you come to Mother Hubbard's pub on the right. **Turn right here A to Smisby, to re-enter Derbyshire.** Smisby church can be seen ahead beyond a couple of broad meadows which were part of the tournament field in medieval times – Sir Walter Scott described a tourney here in *Ivanhoe*. The tall building close to the church is Smisby Hall which dates from early Tudor times. Note the quaint brick lock-up to the right of the road. **At the end of the village turn left on to the B5006 to Ticknall.** This is a pleasant road through undulating farm land. Ticknall is a village which has more than its fair share of beautiful cottages, some built of stone, some of brick.

Turn right at the junction

Melbourne Hall

with the A514 towards Derby.
The car park at Ticknall is to the
left opposite The Wheel pub. A
little further on, the entrance to
Calke Abbey and park is to the
right, just before a graceful bridge
which spans the road (this took a
tramway over the road which
carried limestone from quarries
at Ticknall – a tunnel was built to
hide it from view near the main
gates to the Abbey).

**Ignore the turn to
Melbourne and Staunton
Harold to the right, keeping
on the A514.** Enjoy views of the
Vale of Trent as the road descends
to Stanton by Bridge where it is
joined by the B587 from
Melbourne. Cross the River Trent
over the ancient Swarkestone
Bridge. There is an attractive lake
to the left as the road runs over
the long causeway before
reaching the bridge itself.
Although the main span over the
river was rebuilt in classical style
in 1801, the seventeen arches of
the causeway are original and
were put up about 700 years ago.
Swarkestone Bridge has always
had strategic importance and the
Cavaliers were defeated nearby in
1643. It was the most southerly
point reached by the Scottish
army in 1745.

**Keep to the main road
(A514) after the bridge for
about ¹⁄₂ mile and then turn
right 🅱 to Weston-on-Trent.**
The flood plain of the Trent is rich
and fields of vegetables flourish.
Look to the left as you come into

Weston to see Weston Hall, a very
plain, tall building which was
meant to be twice the size but
work on it was interrupted by the
Civil War and never resumed. The
Ukrainian Settlement is to the
right and is a camp site used by
young Ukrainians as a Youth

Centre. The adjacent old rectory is
now a Ukrainian old people's
home. Many Ukrainians came to
Britain after the Second World
War. Immediately after this there
is a byway on the same side
leading to Weston church.
Because of its isolated position it
is kept locked.

**At Aston-on-Trent turn
right at the main road in the
middle of the village to
Shardlow. At Shardlow the
route meets the A6 – turn
right.** Pass Shardlow church with
its square tower on the right and
the hall (1684–1726) to the left.
Cross the canal and turn left at the
Navigation Inn to visit Shardlow
Wharf which has two pubs and a
public car park and is a
fascinating relic of the canal age.
**Otherwise remain on the
main road to cross the River**

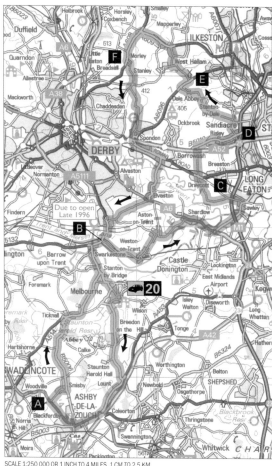

SCALE 1:250 000 OR 1 INCH TO 4 MILES 1 CM TO 2.5 KM

Brick lock-up, Smisby

Trent again, pass the Cavendish Arms pub and come to a roundabout. Take the first exit to Long Eaton on the B6540 going beneath the M1 and passing Sawley Marina. Then the A6 crosses the canal and river once again. Sawley church is to the right as you come to the White Lion and Nag's Head pubs close together on the left. Turn left here before the latter pub on to a road which goes over the motorway. Just after this turn left **C** down Wilne Lane which leads to Church Wilne, a riverside spot which is always popular with anglers. The lane goes on to pass the church, a lovely little building dedicated to St Chad. Like the one at Weston, this is locked. There is a fine lake opposite, made from an abandoned sand and gravel pit. The lane continues close to the river to come into Draycott. **Go straight over the A6005, over a railway and then beneath the A52 to come to the B5010. Turn right to follow the sign towards Sandiacre. The road goes through Risley. When you come to a 30 mph limit turn left D** on to Rushy Lane, where the road is signposted 'Stanton-by-Dale (only)'.

After 3/4 mile, at a staggered crossroads, turn left to Dale Abbey down Noman's Lane. This is a well-hedged country lane, winding through farmland. As you near the village you will see the remaining arch of Dale Abbey standing in a field to the left. Turn left opposite the pub to visit the remarkable parish church, **otherwise continue up Arbour Hill to come to the A6096. Turn right and, after about 1/2 mile, turn left E to Stanley and West Hallam.** The famous Cat and Fiddle windmill, a working post mill, is close to this corner. The road passes a storage depot. **After a sharp left hand bend take the turn to the right to West Hallam and Smalley. This road skirts West Hallam to reach the A609.**

Turn left on to the main

• *PLACES OF INTEREST* •

Elvaston Castle Country Park
The Castle is, in fact, a mansion designed in Gothic style by James Wyatt for the Earl of Harrington and built in 1817, after Wyatt's death. However, for most people the grounds, still being restored by the local council, hold the most interest. They were laid out over a period of more than twenty years by the eccentric Lord Harrington for his wife, a young actress. There are innumerable follies and grottoes including a Moorish temple and splendid Golden Gates. Facilities for visitors to the park include a café, shop, information centre, craft workshops, trail centre, museum, etc. Gypsy caravans, hay wagons and other horse-drawn vehicles are displayed in the castle courtyard. Elvaston was the first country park to be established in England and is open all the year round, from dawn to dusk. Telephone: (01332) 571342.

Melbourne
Nothing remains of the castle built in Norman times. In the fourteenth century the Duke of Bourbon, taken prisoner at Agincourt, was held there for 19 years. Later, when it was suggested that Mary Queen of Scots be imprisoned there, it was thought to be too ruinous. Melbourne church is one of the grandest Norman parish churches in England, and would be even more splendid if the twin towers of the west front had been completed. Building began in the early twelfth century and was largely complete by the beginning of the thirteenth, though the ponderous top of the crossing tower was not added until 1602. Walk past the church towards Melbourne Pool and you will see the south front of the Hall to the left. The house was originally the residence of the Bishops of Carlisle (who held the living of Melbourne) and they subsequently leased it to Sir John Coke, Secretary of State to Charles I. He enlarged the house and the family were later able to buy it. His great-grandson, Sir Thomas Coke, Vice-Chamberlain to both Queen Anne and George I, also added to the building and had the gardens laid out 'to suit with Versailles' by the royal gardeners, George London and Henry Wise. Their plan made much of the small area available and Henry Thorold wrote that there was none more perfect in England. If this is so it is due to the exquisite wrought-iron work by Robert Bakewell, and to the little lead figures of cupids by Jan van Nost which catch the eye at the end of many of the vistas. Van Nost also made the lovely Four Seasons Vase which was the gift of Queen Anne. Melbourne Hall came to the Lamb family by marriage, and they adopted the title of Lord Melbourne in 1770. The second viscount was prime minister at the accession of Queen Victoria, and it was after him that the Australian city was named. Melbourne Hall is now the home of Lord Ralph Kerr.

Melbourne Hall open daily in August (except first and third Mondays) 2–5. Gardens open April–September, Wednesdays, Saturdays, Sundays and Bank Holiday Mondays 2–6. Telephone: (01332) 862502.

Ashby-de-la-Zouch

The distinctive part of the town's name comes from the La Souches, the Norman family who were lords of the manor from c.1160. The fabric of their Norman house was incorporated into the castle, built 1474–76 by the first Lord Hastings. It was besieged for more than a year during the Civil War and finally left in ruins by the Parliamentarians in 1648. In Sir Walter Scott's epic *Ivanhoe*, Ashby is the setting for the confrontation between Ivanhoe and the Black Knight in a spectacular tourney. In reality the tournament field is at the neighbouring village of Smisby. Ashby church has several grandiose tombs and a finger-pillory which was used on those who misbehaved in church.

Morley Church

The wonderful church dates from Norman times and has many interesting medieval tombs and other features. However, its outstanding feature is its medieval glass which came from Dale Abbey and is said to be the best to be found in any parish church in

England. The church is usually open on the first Saturday of the month, 2–4, from April to September inclusive.

Dale Abbey

Only the east end of the church built by Premonasterian monks c.1200 is still standing. Of much greater interest is the tiny village church reached at the end of a cul-de-sac. It adjoins a farmhouse which was once the village pub, and is unique in having pulpit, lectern and clerk's pew behind the altar with box-pews crammed into the rest of the building.

Borrowash. Two more smaller roundabouts follow – go straight over both of them and continue to Borrowash.

By the Noah's Ark pub at Borrowash turn right to Thulston and Elvaston Castle Country Park on the B5010. The road crosses the River Derwent which at this point forms the boundary between Nottinghamshire and Derbyshire. The entrance to the country park is to the right and about a mile further on you come to Thulston village and the A6. Turn right and then take the first turn left to Chellaston.

This lane eventually comes to Chellaston where many new houses are being built. The church is to the left before the lane reaches the A514. In the Middle Ages the quarries here provided alabaster for many monuments to be found in Midlands churches. **At the A514 turn left towards Melbourne, pass by Swarkestone church and the strange 'Summer House' to the left, and cross the medieval bridge again. Keep on the main road after Stanton by Bridge by bearing left to take the B587 to Melbourne and Staunton Harold. Swing right when a road goes ahead towards the East Midlands Airport and keep ahead at a second junction to leave the B587 and return to Melbourne town centre.** ■

road and in 1½ miles come to the A608. Turn left again to follow the sign to Derby and arrive at Morley Smithy, which appropriately has the Three Horseshoes inn. ¼ mile after this, leave the main road by turning left **F** down Church Lane following the sign to Stanley and Chaddesden. Morley church, with medieval glass from Dale Abbey which is said to be the finest to be found in any parish church in England, is reached by a drive to the left.

Continue along the lane which passes the church to come to a crossroads by the King's Corner pub. Go straight over here following a sign to Chaddesden and Spondon. The road skirts the suburbs of Derby with modern housing to the right and (at the

moment) fields to the left. At a roundabout turn left, following the sign to the city centre and Spondon and at the next roundabout turn left again, now taking the A6005 signposted to Borrowash. Keep ahead on this road over the A52 roundabout just after a superstore, still heading for

Staunton Harold

USEFUL ADDRESSES AND INFORMATION

Peak National Park Office

Baslow Road,
Bakewell, Derbyshire DE45 1AE
Tel: (01629) 816200

National Park Information Offices

Bakewell Information Centre
Old Market Hall,
Bridge Street, Bakewell DE45 1DS
Tel: (01629) 813227

Castleton Information Centre
Castle Street (near parish church). Open Easter–October and weekends in winter.
Tel: (01433) 620679

Edale Information Centre
On the right-hand side of the road from the station to the village. Open all year.
Tel: (01433) 670207

Fairholmes Information Centre (Derwent Valley)
Open Easter–October and weekends in winter.
Tel: (01433) 650953

Hartington Old Signal Box
Open in summer at weekends and Bank Holidays.

Langsett (on A616 north west of Sheffield)
Open Easter–October at weekends and Bank Holidays. Sundays only November and December.
Tel: (01226) 370770

Torside (Longdendale)
Open weekends and Bank Holidays Easter–September. Sundays in October.

Tourist Information

Opening times vary – check by telephone

East Midlands Tourist Board
Exchequergate,
Lincoln LN2 1PZ
Tel: (01522) 531521

Ashbourne
13 Market Place,
Ashbourne DE6 1EU
Tel: (01335) 343666

Buxton
The Crescent,
Buxton SK17 6BQ
Tel: (01298) 25106

Chesterfield
Peacock Information Centre,
Low Pavement,
Chesterfield S40 1PB
Tel: (01246) 207777/8

Derby
Assembly Rooms,
Market Place,
Derby DE1 3AH
Tel: (01332) 255802

Glossop
The Gatehouse,
Victoria Street,
Glossop SK13 8HT
Tel: (01457) 855920

Leek
1 Market Place,
Leek ST13 5HH
Tel: (01538) 381000

Matlock Bath
The Pavilion,
Matlock Bath DE4 3NR
Tel: (01629) 55082

Ripley
Town Hall,
Market Place, Ripley DE5 3BT
Tel: (01773) 841488

For information on daily events and weather forecasts

Radio Derby 269m MW and 104.5 FM
Radio Sheffield 1035m MW, 94.7 and 104.1 FM

Weather Forecast
(Weathercall East Midlands)
Tel: (0891) 232782

Other Useful Organisations

The Countryside Commission
John Dower House, Crescent Place, Cheltenham, Gloucestershire GL50 3RA
Tel: (01242) 521381

Ordnance Survey
Romsey Road, Maybush, Southampton SO16 4GU
Tel: 0345 330011 (Lo-call)

National Trust East Midlands Regional Office
Clumber Park Stableyard, Worksop, Notts S80 3BE
Tel: (01909) 486411

English Heritage
Keyston House,
429 Oxford Street,
London W1R 2HD
Tel: (0171) 973 30000

INDEX

Entries in *italic* refer to illustrations.